ENGLAND IN 1685

BEING CHAPTER III OF

THE HISTORY OF ENGLAND

BY

THOMAS BABINGTON MACAULAY

EDITED

WITH NOTES AND AN INTRODUCTION

BY

ARLO BATES

WILDSIDE PRESS

PREFATORY NOTE.

Both for its historical worth and as an introduction to the style of Lord Macaulay the portion of the *History* which is given in the following pages is of much educational value. It is seldom possible to detach from a work so vivid a picture of a period, and to find in the fragment so much the appearance of completeness ; but while it holds its place perfectly in the *History,* this chapter might have been written as an essay, and may be read without any feeling of its being either unfinished or detached.

INTRODUCTION.

I.

Thomas Babington Macaulay was born at Rothley Temple, Leicestershire, England, on October 25, 1800. He came of stout old Scotch Presbyterian stock on his father's side, and on his mother's of Quaker blood. His mother was a woman of strong character and individuality, who, as the boy developed a precocity really amazing, had at once the perception to appreciate his unusual gifts and the good judgment not to spoil him. When hardly more than an infant he showed a remarkable power of writing, producing prose and verse with almost equal facility; but while wonderingly proud, the wise mother had the self-control and sense never to let him see that she regarded his youthful efforts, as she wrote to a friend, "as anything more than a schoolboy's amusement." To her tenderness, her firmness, and her wisdom, Macaulay owed much; and he always regarded her with the warmest affection and admiration.

After four years at an excellent private boarding school, Macaulay entered Trinity College, Cambridge, where he was graduated in 1822. Two years later he took his degree of M.A., and was elected to a fellowship. During all these years his reading was enormous, especially in the line of poetry, fiction, and essays; he exercised himself constantly at the debating clubs then so much in fashion; and he took a keen delight in following the tangled threads of the confused and confusing politics of the day. In connection with the last, the young

man showed that poise and self-command which distinguished
him through life. One biographer says of this period :

A young man of strong passions would, inevitably, have taken
an extreme side — either for reaction or reform. Civil society
seemed threatened by the anarchists ; civil liberty seemed equally
threatened by the Government. . . . Macaulay took his stand, with
the premature prudence and wisdom of a veteran, on the judicious
compromise of sound Whig principles. He was zealous for reform,
but never touched by a breath of revolutionary fervor.

He had by this time begun to be known as a promising
contributor to the magazines, chiefly to Knight's *Quarterly
Magazine*, and among his early pieces the two poems, *The
Battle of Ivry* and *The Battle of Naseby*, are still read. His
work was undoubtedly stimulated and his mind was certainly
developed by the companionship of the brilliant young men
with whom at Cambridge he was in constant association. From
them he received the sympathy which was denied him by his
father, who, always sternly Puritan, became more and more
strenuous in his creed, and so completely occupied with efforts
to promote the abolition of slavery that he neglected his business until he came to actual bankruptcy. Macaulay and his
brother Henry assumed the liabilities their father had incurred,
and for years practically supported the family. Morison says
of him in this connection :

Against Macaulay the author severe things, and as just as
severe, may be said ; but as to his conduct in his own home — as
a son, as a brother, and an uncle — it is only the barest justice to
say that he appears to have touched the farthest verge of human
virtue, sweetness, and generosity.

He gave up cheerfully the prospect of the fortune which he
had expected from his father, and set himself to study for the
bar, to which he was admitted in 1826. He had no inclination
for the law, however, and soon abandoned it for literature.

He had received from Jeffries an invitation to write for the *Edinburgh Review*, and in August, 1825, he contributed to that magazine his essay on Milton. Inferior as is this among the essays of Macaulay, crude and dogmatic as it appears when compared with his riper work, it at once attracted wide attention, and won for the young author praise so warm that he from that minute became a marked man.

It was still the fashion to help on promising young men of literary possibilities with small Civil Service appointments, perhaps quite as much in the hope that their pens might be politically useful as from any disinterested admiration for letters, and in 1829 Macaulay was by Lord Lyndhurst made a Commissioner in Bankruptcy. Two years later he was sent to Parliament to represent the pocket borough of Calne. The seat was in the gift of Lord Lansdowne, who, a stranger, gave it to the young essayist in admiration of his articles on Mill. His first speech in Parliament proved that Macaulay had remarkable oratorical gifts, and he was sent for by the Speaker, who told him " that in all his prolonged experience he had never seen the House in such a state of excitement." His enormous reading, his prodigious memory, his acuteness of mind, his power of clear statement, and the natural gifts as a speaker which he had developed in the debating societies of Cambridge united to produce a wonderful impression.

For four years Macaulay was in Parliament, working with amazing energy, and with rapidly increasing fame. He contributed during this time to the *Edinburgh Review* more than a dozen essays, written in intervals stolen from the time demanded by his public work. He supported a bill to reform the bankruptcy laws which did away with his own office, and as at about this time his Cambridge fellowship also expired he was for a brief period so poor that he was forced to sell the gold medals which he had won at the university. He was soon appointed, however, to the Board of Control, with a comfortable salary.

The place which Macaulay held in the political and in the social world of London was by this time most brilliant and enviable. As an orator, as a man of affairs, and as a literary and social lion, he was equally conspicuous. He had the satisfaction of knowing that the announcement that he was to speak was, in the phrase of Mr. Gladstone, "a summons like a trumpet-call to fill the benches." He recognized clearly, however, that he could not under existing conditions give himself up to any important literary work, and the design of his history was already in his mind. He therefore accepted in 1834 an appointment as legal adviser to the Supreme Council of India, and for four years of exile devoted himself to the onerous duties of that position and to the saving up of a modest competence which would allow him on his return to devote himself to his chosen work.

In India the record of Macaulay was notable both for the enormous amount of work which he accomplished and for the quality of that work. He was not only a Member of the Council, but chairman of two committees of the highest importance, — the Committee of Public Instruction and that which drew up a new Penal Code. His work on the Penal Code was especially valuable, and remains, in the opinion of one biographer, "one of his most durable titles to fame." Certain reforms which he was able to effect were against the interests of some of the English capitalists at that time operating in India, and Macaulay was attacked by them and by the journals in their pay. It is to his honor that notwithstanding the extreme bitterness of these attacks he was throughout the unswerving supporter of the freedom of the press.

Macaulay returned to England in 1838, and in the autumn of the same year made his first visit to Italy. He kept a journal during this trip, and it shows more warmth and enthusiasm than almost anything which his life has left on record. The associations both of classic and of mediæval times were to him thoroughly familiar from his enormous reading and astonishing memory, and it is hardly too much to say that he was more deeply moved by the rich suggestions of Rome than by any purely personal feeling which came into his life.

The next spring found him again in England, and once more in Parliament. He regretted what seemed to him the political necessity of taking office. " I pine for liberty and ease," he wrote, "and freedom of speech and freedom of pen." He was loyal to the Whig party, however, and supported its failing cause. He was made Secretary of War in 1839, and secured personal triumphs, although neither he nor any other man could prevent the fall of Lord Melbourne's government in 1841. This brought to Macaulay the freedom for which he longed. Although he was reëlected as member for Edinburgh, he found himself relieved from the pressure of work, his family and himself comfortably provided for, so that he was not forced to write for money, and had leisure sufficient to allow him to give his most serious efforts to literature. " If I had to choose a lot from all that there are in human life," he wrote at this time to the editor of the *Edinburgh Review*, "I am not sure that I should prefer any to that which has fallen to me."

In 1842 Macaulay published *Lays of Ancient Rome*, and the book was enormously popular. Professor Wilson said of this verse what is perhaps the best that could be said :

A cut-and-thrust style, without any flourish. Scott's style when his blood is up, and the first words come like a vanguard impatient for battle.

Certainly if the reputation of Macaulay had rested only on his verse, he would scarcely have held a high place ; yet the *Lays* are sound, straightforward, and wholesome. If they do not possess great poetic merit, they are at least excellent rhetoric ; they have a directness and simplicity which is always effective.

The great literary work of Macaulay's life, however, was neither the *Lays* nor the *Essays*, but the *History*, of which the first two volumes were published in 1848. He had determined to make history as attractive as fiction, and he succeeded abundantly. Edition after edition was called for, and the author told with amusement of seeing on a placard in the window of a Fleet street bookseller: "Only £2 2s. Hume's *History of England*, in 8 vols. Highly valuable as an introduction to Macaulay." Many were indignant at the way in which church matters were treated, and the Quakers sent to Macaulay a delegation to remonstrate against the manner in which he had dealt with the character of William Penn. Macaulay argued the delegation down ; but it has been proved that he was wrong and they entirely in the right. On the whole, however, the work was received with wonderful applause. Macaulay was in the following year honored by being made Lord Rector of the University of Glasgow, and if he had to endure some sharp criticism, he was solaced with warm praise and the knowledge that no English historian except Gibbon had been so widely read.

Work on the *History*, with some biographies contributed to the *Encyclopedia Britannica*, cover the remaining ten years of Macaulay's life. The third and fourth volumes of the former appeared in 1855, and the fifth volume posthumously. He was created Baron Macaulay of Rothley in 1857, and died December 28, 1859.

II.

The character of Lord Macaulay is neither intricate nor elusive, except in so far as all humanity may be said to be difficult to understand. He was upright, honorable, kindly, self-controlled, and practical. His generosity, his love for children, and his respectful bearing toward his rather trying father, the manliness with which in Parliament he insisted upon preserving the integrity of his personal convictions even at the sacrifice of his political interests, — all entitle him to esteem and admiration.

In society he was noted for his wonderful capacity, and, it may be added, his no less wonderful pertinacity, in talk. His abundant store of knowledge, his facility in embodying this in words, and the activity of his mind gave to his talk amazing richness; but he was unfortunately given to the habit of overriding conversation, and of turning the talk into a monologue. The witty Sydney Smith, whimsically complaining that Macaulay never gave him a chance to get in a word, once said to him, "When I'm gone, you'll be sorry that you never heard me speak." He had, moreover, a somewhat autocratic way of putting forward his opinions that made William Windam declare satirically that he wished he could ever be "as cocksure of anything as Macaulay is of everything." After an illness, when Macaulay was too weak to keep up to his usual level of talk, Sydney Smith said, " Now he has occasional flashes of silence that make his conversation perfectly delightful."

The personal appearance of the historian in 1856 is pleasantly described by Hawthorne in the *English Notebooks*. His first sight of Macaulay was at a breakfast.

He was a man of large presence, — a portly personage, grayhaired, but scarcely yet aged; and his face had a remarkable intelligence, not vivid nor sparkling, but conjoined with great quietude, — and if it gleamed or brightened at one time more than another, it was like the sheen over a broad surface of sea. There was a somewhat careless self-possession, large and broad enough to be called dignity; and the more I looked at him, the more I knew he was a distinguished person, and wondered who.

Lord Macaulay's wonderful memory was the astonishment of his friends, and was perhaps the most remarkable ever possessed by a man of letters. As a boy he was able to repeat almost the whole of *The Lay of the Last Minstrel* after a single reading; when he was fifty-eight years old he learned the four hundred lines of the last act of *The Merchant of Venice* in a couple of hours; and he declared that if all copies of *Paradise Lost* and *Pilgrim's Progress* were to vanish from the earth, he could replace them from memory. Almost every writer who has given reminiscences of him furnishes instances of this power, which was the more remarkable as it seems to have been a direct gift of nature rather than a deliberate acquirement.

His most marked intellectual habit was his practice of unstinted and omnivorous reading. He may indeed be said to have carried this to great excess, and to have read inordinately. The lists which he himself gives of the books, ancient and modern, which he went through are amazing, and confessedly they omit the numerous light works, — often fiction of no literary merit whatever, — of which he devoured quantities. Reading with Macaulay was as near a disease as such a habit can come, and one of his biographers [1] is hardly too severe when he writes :

His acute intellect and nimble fancy are not paired with an emotional endowment of corresponding weight and volume. His endless and aimless reading was the effect, not the cause, of this disposition. . . . This incessant reading was directed by no aim, to no purpose — was prompted by no idea on which he wished to throw light, no thoughtful conception which needed to be verified and tested. Macaulay's omnivorous reading is often referred to as if it were a title to honor; it was far more of the nature of a defect. . . . How dry the inward springs of meditation must have been to allow of such an employment of time!

[1] J. Cotter Morison, in *English Men of Letters* series.

III.

In the style of Macaulay largely lies the secret of his success. When he sent the essay on Milton to the *Edinburgh
Review* Jeffries wrote to him, " The more I think, the less I
can conceive where you picked up that style." Consciously
or unconsciously, he had picked it up largely in the debating
societies at Cambridge, where a natural bent of mind had been
developed and trained. By nature he was gifted with an aptitude for oratory, and this was so increased by frequent and
congenial use throughout his whole career at the university
that it came to a rare perfection.

Macaulay's style is essentially that of the orator. It is
addressed to an audience which is to be reached rather by
superficial form than by finer graces. The rolling, well-rounded
periods, the repetitions which make it easy for the hearer to
follow spoken discourse, the simplicity and directness of statement, the frequent introduction of striking allusions or illus-
trations which keep the attention alert, — all these qualities are
essentially oratorical. They are all to be found admirably
employed in the published speeches of Macaulay; and the
student of style may make an interesting and profitable comparison between the orations delivered in Parliament and what
may almost be called the orations published as essays. The
method is practically the same in both; and in both will be
found practically the same defects and the same virtues.

The defects of an oratorical style are that it is likely to be
limited to those effects which may be produced instantly; that
it is constantly likely to sacrifice lasting to momentary impres-
sions; that it is apt to be confined to ideas and sentiments
which may be conveyed directly, to the exclusion of those
which result from reflection and suggestion. The orator is
constantly exposed to the danger of dealing only with thoughts
and emotions superficial and purely of the moment.

The merits of this method are no less marked than its defects. The power of arresting attention, of awakening interest, of stimulating minds not easily accessible to any form of literature, is conspicuous on every page Macaulay ever wrote. The orator depends much upon cadence and rhythm. He makes of his words an instrument which plays a music not subtle or delicate, it is true, but the more appealing to the popular ear from its very lack of over-refinement. In the street or in the market place a military band is more effective than a string quartette ; and Macaulay chose to be the band. Early in his literary career he said frankly that he put " tinsel " into his articles to please the general public ; and it is at least true that the general public were fascinated. It is impossible not to find in these admirably constructed sentences, in these swinging sonorous periods, an exhilaration which stirs the blood and arouses the mind. A dull writer is almost an immoral one, since he is encouraging an indifference or a repugnance to literature ; and on the other hand we owe no small debt to one who, like Macaulay, fosters the love of reading, awakens an interest in important historical affairs, and calls attention to intellectual problems.

The matter of any writer is closely connected with the manner in which it is presented, and the material with which Macaulay deals might be criticised in terms much the same as those in which his style has been commented upon. Edmund Gosse remarks justly :

English literature has seen no great writer more unspiritual than Macaulay, more unimaginative, more demurely satisfied with the phenomenal aspect of life . . . . Satisfied with surfaces, he observed them with extraordinary liveliness. He preferred to be entertaining, instructive, even exhaustive, on almost every legitimate subject of human thought; but the one thing he never realizes is to be suggestive. What he knows he tells in a clear, positive way ; and he knows so much that often, especially in youth, we desire no other guide ; but he is without vision of unseen things ; he has no message to the heart ; the waters of the soul are never troubled by his copious and admirable flow of information.

This is, however, not quite the whole truth. Macaulay had, it is true, more agility of mind than imagination, and he seldom went beyond the bounds of the matter-of-fact; but he so arranged his material, he so eloquently presented the conditions of the past, as to reach a great audience not to be aroused or held by any other means. Readers not able to follow the more lofty flights of more imaginative writers are delighted and instructed by him. A body of workmen sent to him a vote of thanks for having produced a history so clearly written that persons of their class could understand and enjoy it; and by implication this explains Macaulay's strongest hold upon his public. In thought and in style he is above everything else lucid and easy to follow. He keeps the attention because he never confuses it, never fatigues it, never fails to stimulate it.

IV.

The attitude of Macaulay toward history he has himself stated with admirable clearness. He held that "it should invest with the reality of flesh and blood beings whom we are too much inclined to consider as personified qualities in an allegory; call up our ancestors before us with all their peculiarities of language, manners, and garb; show us their houses, seat us at their tables, rummage their old-fashioned wardrobes, explain the uses of their ponderous furniture." In other words, he held that history, no less than fiction, should be a lively and vivid picture of the actual, warm, human life of the past. He aimed to give to the narrative of real occurrences, to the portrayal of genuine personages, the same life that fiction bestows on the events and characters of fancy. His wish was to make the past, so far as is possible, vital with the reality which informs the life of the present.

His manner of attempting to carry out this really noble conception was that of presenting each character, each state of society, with the utmost detail and with abundant personal incident. In practice such a method is less admirable than it is in theory. The historian necessarily deals with periods of time so great that the detailed account of each personage, of each political intrigue, of every national crisis, is apt to befog the general outlines. The reader gets, indeed, a clear and vivid impression of individual statesmen, or of separate eras, but is less likely to be able out of the multiplicity of images to gain a clear conception of the great movements of history. The very richness of Macaulay's method tended to obscure the sharpness of the outline of the whole. The slow processes of social evolution, the development of political ideals, are lost sight of in the closeness with which the attention is won to regard special periods and marked men.

If his method be allowed, however, it could hardly be handled more satisfactorily. Morison is giving to the historian no more than his due when he says warmly:

Historical narrative in his hands is something vastly more complex and involved than it ever was before. . . . Beneath the smooth and polished surface layer under layer may be seen of subordinate narratives, crossing and interlacing each other like the parts in the score of an oratorio. And this complexity results not in confusion but in the most admirable clearness and unity of effect. His pages are not only pictorial, they are dramatic. Scene is made to follow scene with the skill of an accomplished playwright; and each has been planned and fashioned with a view to its thoroughly prepared place in the whole piece. . . . Many writers before Macaulay had done their best to be graphic and picturesque, but none ever saw that the scattered fragments of truth could, by incessant toil directed by the artistic eye, be worked into a mosaic which for color, freedom, and finish might rival the creations of fancy.

The defects of the *History*, however, cannot be passed over in silence. Whether the effort to make his account of other times share the attractiveness of fiction led the historian perilously near to the attitude of the novelist who feels himself at liberty to represent his characters as he pleases, or whether the oratorical habit of feeling that the effective rounding of a period is almost a moral necessity betrayed him into misstatements, certain it is that Macaulay did now and again distort fact and misrepresent character. The extent of his inaccuracy has perhaps been exaggerated, since inaccuracy is the fault which is least likely to be forgiven to a historian; but the list of charges which might be made out is still sufficiently grave. It is often necessary to correct his statements, as it is also needful to gain a general outline, from some other author; but the other and more accurate authors will almost always be most strikingly lacking in the life and freshness which in his pages never fail.

The selection which is published in the following pages, the third chapter of the first volume of the *History*, is a striking example of Macaulay's power of handling a great mass of details and of producing from them a result which is most admirably readable. The picture of life in England in the late seventeenth century is made up of a wonderfully large number of details, but they are so well arranged, one statement is so linked with others, all are so completely woven together, that the attention of the reader is held closely throughout, and the impression produced by the whole has the freshness of an account of present affairs rather than the formality and remoteness which generally belong to such a summary. The reader feels rather that he is learning the condition of some country which he might to-day visit, than that he is studying of things as they existed centuries ago.

It is true that Macaulay does not go much below the surface. He does not concern himself with the causes which make the country into which he takes us what it is ; but at least he does take us there, and that with a completeness and a clearness which other historians have in vain tried to rival. It is not as if we were mere students, it is as if by some magic we had been transported to England in the times of Charles II, and were with our own eyes observing the particulars which the historian has accumulated from sources so numerous and so diverse.

ENGLAND IN 1685.

I INTEND, in this chapter, to give a description of the state
in which England was at the time when the crown passed
from Charles the Second to his brother.[1] Such a description,
composed from scanty and dispersed materials, must necessarily be very imperfect. Yet it may perhaps correct some 5
false notions which would render the subsequent narrative
unintelligible or uninstructive.

If we would study with profit the history of our ancestors,
we must be constantly on our guard against that delusion
which the well-known names of families, places, and offices 10
naturally produce, and must never forget that the country of
which we read was a very different country from that in
which we live. In every experimental science there is a
tendency towards perfection. In every human being there
is a wish to ameliorate his own condition. These two prin- 15
ciples have often sufficed, even when counteracted by great
public calamities and by bad institutions, to carry civilization
rapidly forward. No ordinary misfortune, no ordinary misgovernment, will do so much to make a nation wretched, as
the constant progress of physical knowledge and the constant 20
effort of every man to better himself will do to make a nation
prosperous. It has often been found that profuse expenditure, heavy taxation, absurd commercial restrictions, corrupt
tribunals, disastrous wars, seditions, persecutions, conflagra-
tions, inundations, have not been able to destroy capital so 25
fast as the exertions of private citizens have been able to

create it. It can easily be proved that, in our own land, the
national wealth has, during at least six centuries, been almost
uninterruptedly increasing; that it was greater under the
Tudors than under the Plantagenets; that it was greater
5 under the Stuarts than under the Tudors;[2] that, in spite of
battles, sieges, and confiscations, it was greater on the day
of the Restoration than on the day when the Long Parliament met;[3] that, in spite of maladministration, of extravagance, of public bankruptcy, of two costly and unsuccessful
10 wars, of the pestilence, and of the fire, it was greater on the
day of the death of Charles the Second than on the day of
his restoration.   This progress, having continued during
many ages, became at length, about the middle of the eighteenth century, portentously rapid, and has proceeded, during
15 the nineteenth, with accelerated velocity.   In consequence
partly of our geographical and partly of our moral position,
we have, during several generations, been exempt from evils
which have elsewhere impeded the efforts and destroyed the
fruits of industry.   While every part of the Continent, from
20 Moscow to Lisbon, has been the theatre of bloody and
devastating wars, no hostile standard has been seen here but
as a trophy.   While revolutions have taken place all around
us, our government has never once been subverted by violence.   During a hundred years there has been in our island
25 no tumult of sufficient importance to be called an insurrection.   The law has never been borne down either by popular
fury or by regal tyranny.   Public credit has been held sacred.
The administration of justice has been pure.   Even in times
which might by Englishmen be justly called evil times, we
30 have enjoyed what almost every other nation in the world
would have considered as an ample measure of civil and
religious freedom.   Every man has felt entire confidence that
the state would protect him in the possession of what had
been earned by his diligence and hoarded by his self-denial.

Under the benignant influence of peace and liberty, science has flourished, and has been applied to practical purposes on a scale never before known.   The consequence is, that a change to which the history of the old world furnishes no parallel has taken place in our country.   Could the England 5 of 1685 be, by some magical process, set before our eyes, we should not know one landscape in a hundred or one building in ten thousand.   The country gentleman would not recognize his own fields.   The inhabitant of the town would not recognize his own street.   Everything has been changed 10 but the great features of nature, and a few massive and durable works of human art.   We might find out Snowdon and Windermere, the Cheddar Cliffs and Beachy Head.   We might find out here and there a Norman minster, or a castle which witnessed the Wars of the Roses.   But, with such rare 15 exceptions, everything would be strange to us.   Many thousands of square miles which are now rich corn land and meadow, intersected by green hedgerows, and dotted with villages and pleasant country-seats, would appear as moors overgrown with furze, or fens abandoned to wild ducks.   We should see 20 straggling huts built of wood and covered with thatch where we now see manufacturing towns and seaports renowned to the farthest ends of the world.   The capital itself would shrink to dimensions not much exceeding those of its present suburb on the south of the Thames.   Not less strange to us 25 would be the garb and manners of the people, the furniture and the equipages, the interior of the shops and dwellings. Such a change in the state of a nation seems to be at least as well entitled to the notice of an historian as any change of the dynasty or of the ministry.   30

One of the first objects of an inquirer who wishes to form a correct notion of the state of a community at a given time must be to ascertain of how many persons that community then consisted.   Unfortunately the population of England in

1685 cannot be ascertained with perfect accuracy.   For no
great state had then adopted the wise course of periodically
numbering the people.   All men were left to conjecture for
themselves; and, as they generally conjectured without ex-
5 amining facts, and under the influence of strong passions
and prejudices, their guesses were often ludicrously absurd.
Even intelligent Londoners ordinarily talked of London as
containing several millions of souls.   It was confidently
asserted by many that, during the thirty-five years which had
10 elapsed between the accession of Charles the First and the
Restoration, the population of the city had increased by two
millions.   Even while the ravages of the plague and fire[4]
were recent, it was the fashion to say that the capital still
had a million and a half of inhabitants.   Some persons, dis-
15 gusted by these exaggerations, ran violently into the opposite
extreme.   Thus Isaac Vossius, a man of undoubted parts
and learning, strenuously maintained that there were only
two millions of human beings in England, Scotland, and
Ireland taken together.
20   We are not, however, left without the means of correcting
the wild blunders into which some minds were hurried by
national vanity, and others by a morbid love of paradox.
There are extant three computations which seem to be entitled to peculiar attention.   They are entirely independent of
25 each other: they proceed on different principles, and yet
there is little difference in the results.
    One of these computations was made in the year 1696 by
Gregory King, Lancaster herald, a political arithmetician of
great acuteness and judgment.   The basis of his calculations
30 was the number of houses returned in 1690 by the officers
who made the last collection of the hearth money.   The conclusion at which he arrived was, that the population of England
was nearly five millions and a half.
    About the same time King William the Third was desirous

to ascertain the comparative strength of the religious sects
into which the community was divided.   An inquiry was
instituted; and reports were laid before him from all the
dioceses of the realm.   According to these reports the number of his English subjects must have been about five million   5
two hundred thousand.*

Lastly, in our own days, Mr. Finlaison, an actuary[5] of
eminent skill, subjected the ancient parochial registers to all
the tests which the modern improvements in statistical science enabled him to apply.   His opinion was that, at the   10
close of the seventeenth century, the population of England
was a little under five million two hundred thousand souls.

Of these three estimates, framed without concert by different persons from different sets of materials, the highest,
which is that of King, does not exceed the lowest, which is   15
that of Finlaison, by one-twelfth.   We may, therefore, with
confidence pronounce that when James the Second reigned,
England contained between five million and five million five
hundred thousand inhabitants.   On the very highest suppo-
sition she then had less than one-third of her present popu-   20
lation, and less than three times the population which is now
collected in her gigantic capital.

The increase of the people has been great in every part
of the kingdom, but generally much greater in the northern
than in the southern shires.   In truth a large part of the   25
country beyond Trent was, down to the eighteenth century,
in a state of barbarism.   Physical and moral causes had
concurred to prevent civilization from spreading to that
region.   The air was inclement; the soil was generally such

---

* The practice of reckoning the population by sects was long fashion-   30
able. Gulliver says of the king of Brobdingnag, " He laughed at my
odd arithmetic, as he was pleased to call it, in reckoning the numbers of
our people by a computation drawn from the several sects among us in
religion and politics."

as required skillful and industrious cultivation ; and there
could be little skill or industry in a tract which was often
the theatre of war, and which, even when there was nominal
peace, was constantly desolated by bands of Scottish
5 marauders.   Before the union of the two British crowns,
and long after that union, there was as great a difference
between Middlesex and Northumberland as there now is
between Massachusetts and the settlements of those squatters who, far to the west of the Mississippi, administer a
10 rude justice with the rifle and the dagger.[6]   In the reign of
Charles the Second, the traces left by ages of slaughter and
pillage were still distinctly perceptible, many miles south of
the Tweed, in the face of the country and in the lawless
manners of the people.   There was still a large class of
15 moss-troopers,[7] whose calling was to plunder dwellings and
to drive away whole herds of cattle.   It was found necessary,
soon after the Restoration, to enact laws of great severity
for the prevention of these outrages.   The magistrates of
Northumberland and Cumberland were authorized to raise
20 bands of armed men for the defence of property and order ;
and provision was made for meeting the expense of these
levies by local taxation.   The parishes were required to keep
bloodhounds for the purpose of hunting the freebooters.
Many old men who were living in the middle of the eigh-
25 teenth century could well remember the time when those
ferocious dogs were common.   Yet, even with such auxiliaries,
it was often found impossible to track the robbers to their
retreats among the hills and morasses.   For the geography
of that wild country was very imperfectly known.   Even
30 after the accession of George the Third,[8] the path over the
fells from Borrowdale to Ravenglas was still a secret carefully kept by the dalesmen, some of whom had probably in
their youth escaped from the pursuit of justice by that road.
The seats of the gentry and the larger farmhouses were

fortified. Oxen were penned at night beneath the over-
hanging battlements of the residence, which was known by
the name of the Peel. The inmates slept with arms at their
sides. Huge stones and boiling water were in readiness to
crush and scald the plunderer who might venture to assail 5
the little garrison. No traveler ventured into that country
without making his will. The judges on circuit, with the
whole body of barristers, attorneys, clerks, and serving men,
rode on horseback from Newcastle to Carlisle, armed and
escorted by a strong guard under the command of the 10
sheriffs. It was necessary to carry provisions, for the country was a wilderness which afforded no supplies. The spot
where the cavalcade halted to dine, under an immense oak,
is not yet forgotten. The irregular vigor with which criminal justice was administered shocked observers whose life 15
had been passed in more tranquil districts. Juries, animated
by hatred and by a sense of common danger, convicted
house-breakers and cattle-stealers with the promptitude of a
court-martial in a mutiny; and the convicts were hurried by
scores to the gallows. Within the memory of some who are 20
still living, the sportsman who wandered in pursuit of game
to the sources of the Tyne, found the heaths round Keeldar
Castle peopled by a race scarcely less savage than the Indians
of California, and heard with surprise the half-naked women
chanting a wild measure, while the men with brandished 25
dirks danced a war dance.[9]

Slowly and with difficulty peace was established on the
border. In the train of peace came industry and all the arts
of life. Meanwhile it was discovered that the regions north
of the Trent possessed in their coal beds a source of wealth 30
far more precious than the gold mines of Peru. It was
found that in the neighborhood of these beds almost every
manufacture might be most profitably carried on. A constant stream of emigrants began to roll northward. It

appeared, by the returns of 1841, that the ancient archiepis-
copal province of York contained two-sevenths of the population of England. At the time of the Revolution that
province was believed‚ to contain only one-seventh of the
5 population.   In Lancashire, the number of inhabitants
appears to have increased ninefold, while in Norfolk,
Suffolk, and Northamptonshire, it has hardly doubled.*

Of the taxation we can speak with more confidence and
precision than of the population.   The revenue of England,
10 under Charles the Second, was small, when compared with
the resources which she even then possessed, or with the
sums which were raised by the governments of the neighboring countries.   It was little more than three-fourths of the
revenue of the United Provinces, and was hardly one-fifth of
15 the revenue of France.

The most important head of receipt was the excise, which,
in the last year of the reign of Charles, produced five hundred and eighty-five thousand pounds, clear of all deductions.
The net proceeds of the customs amounted in the same year
20 to five hundred and thirty thousand pounds. These burdens
did not lie very heavy on the nation. The tax on chimneys,[10]
though less productive, raised far louder murmurs.   The
discontent excited by direct imposts is, indeed, almost always
out of proportion to the quantity of money which they bring
25 into the Exchequer; and the tax on chimneys was, even
among direct imposts, peculiarly odious ; for it could be
levied only by means of domiciliary visits, and of such visits
the English have always been impatient to a degree which
the people of other countries can but faintly conceive. The
30 poorer householders were frequently unable to pay their

---

* I do not, of course, pretend to strict accuracy here ; but I believe
that whoever will take the trouble to compare the last returns of hearth
money in the reign of William the Third with the census of 1841 will
come to a conclusion not very different from mine.

hearth money to the day. When this happened, their furniture was distrained without mercy; for the tax was farmed
and a farmer of taxes is, of all creditors, proverbially the
most rapacious. The collectors were loudly accused of per-
forming their unpopular duty with harshness and insolence. 5
It was said that as soon as they appeared at the threshold
of a cottage, the children began to wail, and the old women
ran to hide their earthenware. Nay, the single bed of a
poor family had sometimes been carried away and sold.
The net annual receipt from this tax was two hundred 10
thousand pounds.*

When to the three great sources of income which have
been mentioned we add the royal domains, then far more
extensive than at present, the first fruits and tenths, which
had not yet been surrendered to the Church, the duchies of 15
Cornwall and Lancaster, the forfeitures and the fines, we shall
find that the whole annual revenue of the crown may be
fairly estimated at about fourteen hundred thousand pounds.

* There are, in the Pepysian Library, some ballads of that age on
the chimney money. I will give a specimen or two :   20

   "The good old dames, whenever they the chimney man espied,
    Unto their nooks they haste away, their pots and pipkins hide.
    There is not one old dame in ten, and search the nation through,
    But, if you talk of chimney men, will spare a curse or two."

Again :   25
     "Like plundering soldiers they'd enter the door,
     And make a distress on the goods of the poor,
     While frighted poor children distractedly cried :
     This nothing abated their insolent pride."

   In the British Museum there are doggerel verses composed on the 30
same subject and in the same spirit :

      "Or if through poverty it be not paid,
      For cruelty to tear away the single bed,
      On which the poor man rests his weary head,
      At once deprives him of his rest and bread."   35

Of the post office, more will hereafter be said.   The profits
of that establishment had been appropriated by parliament
to the Duke of York.

The king's revenue was, or rather ought to have been,
5 charged with the payment of about eighty thousand pounds
a year, the interest of the sum fraudulently detained in the
Exchequer by the Cabal.[11]   While Danby[12] was at the head
of the finances, the creditors had received their dividends,
though not with the strict punctuality of modern times; but
10 those who had succeeded him at the treasury had been less
expert, or less solicitous to maintain public faith.   Since the
victory won by the court over the Whigs, not a farthing had
been paid; and no redress was granted to the sufferers, till
a new dynasty had established a new system.   There can
15 be no greater error than to imagine that the device of meeting the exigencies of the state by loans was imported into
our island by William the Third.   From a period of imme-
morial antiquity it had been the practice of every English
government to contract debts.   What the Revolution[13]
20 introduced was the practice of honestly paying them.

By plundering the public creditor, it was possible to make
an income of about fourteen hundred thousand pounds, with
some occasional help from France, support the necessary
charges of the government and the wasteful expenditure of
25 the court.   For that load which pressed most heavily on the
finances of the great continental states was here scarcely
felt.   In France, Germany, and the Netherlands, armies,
such as Henry the Fourth and Philip the Second[14] had
never employed in time of war, were kept up in the midst
30 of peace.   Bastions and ravelins were everywhere rising,
constructed on principles unknown to Parma[15] or Spinola.[16]
Stores of artillery and ammunition were accumulated, such
as even Richelieu,[17] whom the preceding generation had
regarded as a worker of prodigies, would have pronounced

fabulous. No man could journey many leagues in those countries without hearing the drums of a regiment on march, or being challenged by the sentinels on the draw-bridge of a fortress. In our island, on the contrary, it was possible to live long and to travel far without being once 5 reminded, by any martial sight or sound, that the defence of nations had become a science and a calling. The majority of Englishmen who were under twenty-five years of age had probably never seen a company of regular soldiers. Of the cities which, in the Civil War, had valiantly repelled hostile 10 armies, scarce one was now capable of sustaining a siege. The gates stood open night and day. The ditches were dry. The ramparts had been suffered to fall into decay, or were repaired only that the townsfolk might have a pleasant walk on summer evenings. Of the old baronial keeps many had 15 been shattered by the cannon of Fairfax and Cromwell,[18] and lay in heaps of ruin, overgrown with ivy. Those which remained had lost their martial character, and were now rural palaces of the aristocracy. The moats were turned into preserves of carp and pike. The mounds were planted 20 with fragrant shrubs, through which spiral walks ran up to summer houses adorned with mirrors and paintings. There were still to be seen, on the capes of the seacoast and on many inland hills, tall posts, surmounted by barrels. Once those barrels had been filled with pitch. Watchmen had 25 been set round them in seasons of danger; and, within a few hours after a Spanish sail had been discovered in the chan-nel, or after a thousand Scottish moss-troopers had crossed the Tweed, the signal fires were blazing fifty miles off, and whole counties were rising in arms. But many years had 30 now elapsed since the beacons had been lighted, and they were regarded rather as curious relics of ancient manners than as parts of a machinery necessary to the safety of the state.

The only army which the law recognized was the militia. That force had been remodeled by two acts of parliament passed shortly after the Restoration. Every man who possessed five hundred pounds a year derived from land, or six
5 thousand pounds of personal estate, was bound to provide, equip, and pay, at his own charge, one horseman. Every man who had fifty pounds a year, derived from land, or six hundred pounds of personal estate, was charged in like manner with one pikeman or musketeer. Smaller proprietors
10 were joined together in a kind of society, for which our language does not afford a special name, but which an Athenian would have called a Synteleia; and each society was required to furnish, according to its means, a horse soldier or a foot soldier. The whole number of cavalry and infantry thus
15 maintained was popularly estimated at a hundred and thirty thousand men.

The king was, by the ancient constitution of the realm, and by the recent and solemn acknowledgment of both Houses of parliament, the sole captain-general of this large
20 force. The lords lieutenants and their deputies held the command under him, and appointed meetings for drilling and inspection. The time occupied by such meetings, however, was not to exceed fourteen days in one year. The justices of the peace were authorized to inflict slight penal-
25 ties for breaches of discipline. Of the ordinary cost no part was paid by the crown; but, when the trainbands were called out against an enemy, their subsistence became a charge on the general revenue of the state, and they were subject to the utmost rigor of martial law.
30   There were those who looked on the militia with no friendly eye. Men who had traveled much on the Continent, who had marveled at the stern precision with which every sentinel moved and spoke in the citadels built by Vauban,[19] who had seen the mighty armies which poured

along all the roads of Germany to chase the Ottoman from
the gates of Vienna, and who had been dazzled by the well-
ordered pomp of the household troops of Louis,[20] sneered
much at the way in which the peasants of Devonshire and
Yorkshire marched and wheeled, shouldered muskets, and 5
ported pikes. The enemies of the liberties and religion of
England looked with aversion on a force which could not,
without extreme risk, be employed against those liberties and
that religion, and missed no opportunity of throwing ridicule
on the rustic soldiery.* Enlightened patriots, when they 10
contrasted these rude levies with the battalions which, in
time of war, a few hours might bring to the coast of Kent
or Sussex, were forced to acknowledge that, dangerous as it
might be to keep up a permanent military establishment, it
might be more dangerous still to stake the honor and inde- 15
pendence of the country on the result of a contest between
ploughmen officered by justices of the peace, and veteran
warriors led by marshals of France. In parliament, however,
it was necessary to express such opinions with some reserve,
for the militia was an institution eminently popular. Every 20
reflection thrown on it excited the indignation of both the
great parties in the state, and especially of that party which

* Dryden, in his *Cymon and Iphigenia*, expressed, with his usual
keenness and energy, the sentiments which had been fashionable among
the sycophants of James the Second: 25

> " The country rings around with loud alarms,
> And raw in fields the rude militia swarms;
> Mouths without hands, maintained at vast expense,
> In peace a charge, in war a weak defence.
> Stout once a month they march, a blustering band, 30
> And ever, but in time of need, at hand.
> This was the morn when, issuing on the guard,
> Drawn up in rank and file, they stood prepared
> Of seeming arms to make a short essay,
> Then hasten to be drunk, the business of the day." 35

was distinguished by peculiar zeal for monarchy and for the
Anglican Church. The array of the counties was commanded
almost exclusively by Tory noblemen and gentlemen. They
were proud of their military rank, and considered an insult
5 offered to the service to which they belonged as offered to
themselves. They were also perfectly aware that whatever
was said against a militia was said in favor of a standing
army; and the name of standing army was hateful to them.
One such army had held dominion in England; and under
10 that dominion the king had been murdered, the nobility
degraded, the landed gentry plundered, the Church persecuted. There was scarce a rural grandee who could not
tell a story of wrongs and insults suffered by himself or by
his father, at the hands of the parliamentary soldiers. One
15 old Cavalier had seen half his manor house blown up. The
hereditary elms of another had been hewn down. A third
could never go into his parish church without being reminded,
by the defaced scutcheons and headless statues of his ances-
try, that Oliver's redcoats had once stabled their horses
20 there.[21] The consequence was that those very royalists who
were most ready to fight for the king themselves were the
last persons whom he could venture to ask for the means of
hiring regular troops.

Charles, however, had, a few months after his restoration,
25 begun to form a small standing army. He felt that, without
some better protection than that of the trainbands and beef-
eaters, his palace and person would hardly be secure in the
vicinity of a great city swarming with warlike fifth-monarchy[22]
men who had just been disbanded. He therefore, careless
30 and profuse as he was, contrived to spare from his pleasures
a sum sufficient to keep up a body of guards. With the
increase of trade and of public wealth his revenues increased;
and he was thus enabled, in spite of the occasional murmurs
and remonstrances of the Commons, to make gradual addi-

tions to his regular forces. One considerable addition was made a few months before the close of his reign. The costly, useless, and pestilential settlement of Tangier was abandoned to the barbarians who dwelt around it ; and the garrison, consisting of one regiment of horse and two 5 regiments of foot, was brought to England.

The little army thus formed by Charles the Second was the germ of that great and renowned army which has, in the present century, marched triumphant into Madrid and Paris, into Canton and Candahar. The Life Guards, who now 10 form two regiments, were then distributed into three troops, each of which consisted of two hundred carabineers, exclusive of officers. This corps, to which the safety of the king and royal family was confided, had a very peculiar character. Even the privates were designated as gentlemen of the guard. 15 Many of them were of good families, and had held commissions in the Civil War. Their pay was far higher than that of the most favored regiment of our time, and would in that age have been thought a respectable provision for the younger son of a country gentleman. Their fine horses, their rich 20 housings, their cuirasses, and their buff coats adorned with ribbons, velvet, and gold lace made a splendid appearance in St. James's Park. A small body of grenadier dragoons, who came from a lower class and received lower pay, was attached to each troop. Another body of household cavalry 25 distinguished by blue coats and cloaks, and still called the Blues, was generally quartered in the neighborhood of the capital. Near the capital lay also the corps which is now designated as the first regiment of dragoons, but which was then the only regiment of dragoons on the English establish- 30 ment. It had recently been formed out of the cavalry who had returned from Tangier. A single troop of dragoons, which did not form part of any regiment, was stationed near Berwick, for the purpose of keeping the peace among the moss-troopers of the border. For this species of service the dragoon was then thought to be peculiarly qualified. He has since become a mere horse soldier. But in the seventeenth century he was accurately described by Montecuculi 5 as a foot soldier who used a horse only in order to arrive with more speed at the place where military service was to be performed.

The household infantry consisted of two regiments, which were then, as now, called the first regiment of Foot Guards 10 and the Coldstream Guards. They generally did duty near Whitehall and St. James's Palace. As there were then no barracks, and as, by the Petition of Right, they could not be quartered on private families, they filled all the alehouses of Westminster and the Strand.

15 There were five other regiments of foot. One of these, called the Admiral's Regiment, was especially destined to service on board of the fleet. The remaining four still rank as the first four regiments of the line. Two of these represented two bands which had long sustained on the Continent 20 the fame of English valor. The first, or Royal Regiment, had, under the great Gustavus, borne a conspicuous part in the deliverance of Germany. The third regiment, distinguished by flesh-colored facings, from which it derived the well-known name of the Buffs, had, under Maurice of Nas-25 sau,[23] fought not less bravely for the deliverance of the Netherlands. Both these gallant brigades had at length, after many vicissitudes, been recalled from foreign service by Charles the Second, and had been placed on the English establishment.

30 The regiments which now rank as the second and fourth of the line had, in 1685, just returned from Tangier, bringing with them cruel and licentious habits, contracted in a long course of warfare with the Moors. A few companies of infantry which had not been regimented lay in garrison at

Tilbury Fort, at Portsmouth, at Plymouth, and at some other important stations on or near the coast.

Since the beginning of the seventeenth century a great change had taken place in the arms of the infantry. The pike had been gradually giving place to the musket; and at 5 the close of the reign of Charles the Second, most of his foot were musketeers. Still, however, there was a large intermixture of pikemen. Each class of troops was occasionally instructed in the use of the weapon which peculiarly belonged to the other class. Every foot soldier had at his side a 10 sword for close fight. The dragoon was armed like a musketeer, and was also provided with a weapon, which had, during many years, been gradually coming into use, and which the English then called a dagger, but which, from the time of our Revolution, has been known among us by the French 15 name of bayonet. The bayonet seems not to have been so formidable an instrument of destruction as it has since become, for it was inserted in the muzzle of the gun; and in action much time was lost while the soldier unfixed his bayonet in order to fire, and fixed it again in order 20 to charge.

The regular army which was kept up in England at the beginning of the year 1685 consisted, all ranks included, of about seven thousand foot and about seventeen hundred cavalry and dragoons. The whole charge amounted to 25 about two hundred and ninety thousand pounds a year, less than a tenth part of what the military establishment of France then cost in time of peace. The daily pay of a private in the Life Guards was four shillings, in the Blues two shillings and sixpence, in the Dragoons eighteenpence, 30 in the Foot Guards tenpence, and in the line eightpence. The discipline was lax, and indeed could not be otherwise. The common law of England knew nothing of courts-martial, and made no distinction, in time of peace. between

a soldier and any other subject; nor could the government
then venture to ask even the most loyal parliament for a
mutiny bill.   A soldier, therefore, by knocking down his
colonel, incurred only the ordinary penalties of assault and
5 battery, and by refusing to obey orders, by sleeping
on guard, or by deserting his colors, incurred no legal
penalty at all. Military punishments were doubtless inflicted
during the reign of Charles the Second; but they were
inflicted very sparingly, and in such a manner as not to
10 attract public notice or to produce an appeal to the courts
of Westminster Hall.

Such an army as has been described was not very likely
to enslave five millions of Englishmen.   It would indeed
have been hardly able to suppress an insurrection in London
15 if the trainbands of the city had joined the insurgents. Nor
could the king expect that, if a rising took place in England,
he would be able to obtain help from his other dominions.
For, though both Scotland and Ireland supported separate
military establishments, those establishments were not more
20 than sufficient to keep down the Puritan malcontents of the
former kingdom, and the Popish malcontents of the latter.
The government had, however, an important military resource which must not be left unnoticed. There were in the
pay of the United Provinces six fine regiments, formerly
25 commanded by the brave Ossory.[24]   Of these regiments
three had been raised in England and three in Scotland.
Their native prince had reserved to himself the power of
recalling them, if he needed their help against a foreign
or domestic enemy.   In the meantime they were maintained
30 without any charge to him, and were kept under an excellent
discipline, to which he could not have ventured to subject
them.

If the jealousy of the parliament and of the nation made
it impossible for the king to maintain a formidable standing

army, no similar impediment prevented him from making
England the first of maritime powers.   Both Whigs and
Tories were ready to applaud every step tending to increase
the efficiency of that force which, while it was the best protection of the island against foreign enemies, was powerless 5
against civil liberty.   All the greatest exploits achieved
within the memory of that generation by English soldiers had
been achieved in war against English princes.   The victories
of our sailors had been won over foreign foes, and had
averted havoc and rapine from our own soil.   By at least 10
half the nation the battle of Naseby[25] was remembered with
horror, and the battle of Dunbar[26] with pride checkered by
many painful feelings; but the defeat of the Armada,[27] and
the encounters of Blake[28] with the Hollanders and Spaniards
were recollected with unmixed exultation by all parties. 15
Ever since the Restoration, the Commons, even when most
discontented and most parsimonious, had always been
bountiful even to profusion where the interest of the navy
was concerned.   It had been represented to them, while
Danby was minister, that many of the vessels in the royal 20
fleet were old and unfit for sea; and, although the House
was, at that time, in no giving mood, an aid of near six
hundred thousand pounds had been granted for the building
of thirty new men-of-war.

But the liberality of the nation had been made fruitless by 25
the vices of the government.   The list of the king's ships,
it is true, looked well.   There were nine first rates, fourteen
second rates, thirty-nine third rates, and many smaller vessels.   The first rates, indeed, were less than the third rates
of our time ; and the third rates would not now rank as very 30
large frigates.   This force, however, if it had been efficient,
would in those days have been regarded by the greatest
potentate as formidable.   But it existed only on paper.
When the reign of Charles terminated, his navy had sunk·

into degradation and decay, such as would be almost incredible if it were not certified to us by the independent and concurring evidence of witnesses whose authority is beyond exception. Pepys,[29] the ablest man in the English admiralty, 5 drew up, in the year 1684, a memorial on the state of his department, for the information of Charles. A few months later Bonrepaux, the ablest man in the French admiralty, having visited England for the especial purpose of ascertaining her maritime strength, laid the result of his inquiries 10 before Louis. The two reports are to the same effect. Bonrepaux declared that he found everything in disorder and in miserable condition, that the superiority of the French marine was acknowledged with shame and envy at Whitehall, and that the state of our shipping and dockyards was 15 of itself a sufficient guarantee that we should not meddle in the disputes of Europe. Pepys informed his master that the naval administration was a prodigy of wastefulness, corruption, ignorance, and indolence, that no estimate could be trusted, that no contract was performed, that no check was 20 enforced. The vessels which the recent liberality of parliament had enabled the government to build, and which had never been out of harbor, had been made of such wretched timber that they were more unfit to go to sea than the old hulls which had been battered thirty years before by Dutch 25 and Spanish broadsides. Some of the new men-of-war, indeed, were so rotten that, unless speedily repaired, they would go down at their moorings. The sailors were paid with so little punctuality that they were glad to find some usurer who would purchase their tickets at forty per cent 30 discount. The commanders who had not powerful friends at court were even worse treated. Some officers to whom large arrears were due, after vainly importuning the government during many years, had died for want of a morsel of bread.

Most of the ships which were afloat were commanded by men who had not been bred to the sea. This, it is true, was not an abuse introduced by the government of Charles. No state, ancient or modern, had, before that time, made a complete separation between the naval and military services. In the great civilized nations of the old world, Cimon and Lysander, Pompey and Agrippa [30] had fought battles by sea as well as by land. Nor had the impulse which nautical science received at the close of the fifteenth century produced any material improvement in the division of labor. At Flodden [31] the right wing of the victorious army was led by the admiral of England. At Jarnac and Moncontour [32] the Huguenot ranks were marshaled by the admiral of France.[33] Neither John of Austria,[34] the conqueror of Lepanto, nor Lord Howard of Effingham,[35] to whose direction the marine of England was intrusted when the Spanish invaders were approaching our shores, had received the education of a sailor. Raleigh,[36] highly celebrated as a naval commander, had served during many years as a soldier in France, the Netherlands, and Ireland. Blake had distinguished himself by his skillful and valiant defence of an inland town before he humbled the pride of Holland and of Castile on the ocean. Since the Restoration the same system had been followed. Great fleets had been intrusted to the direction of Rupert and Monk,[37] Rupert, who was renowned chiefly as a hot and daring cavalry officer, and Monk, who, when he wanted his ship to tack to larboard, moved the mirth of his crew by calling out, " Wheel to the left."

But about this time wise men began to perceive that the rapid improvement, both of the art of war and of the art of navigation, made it necessary to draw a line between two professions which had hitherto been confounded. Either the command of a regiment or the command of a ship was now a matter quite sufficient to occupy the attention of a

single mind. In the year 1672 the French government
determined to educate young men of good family from a
very early age specially for the sea service. But the English
government, instead of following this excellent example, not
5 only continued to distribute high naval commands among
landsmen, but selected for such commands landsmen who,
even on land, could not safely have been put in any important trust. Any lad of noble birth, any dissolute courtier,
for whom one of the king's mistresses would speak a word,
10 might hope that a ship of the line, and with it the honor of
the country and the lives of hundreds of brave men, would
be committed to his care. It mattered not that he had
never in his life taken a voyage except on the Thames, that
he could not keep his feet in a breeze, that he did not
15 know the difference between latitude and longitude. No
previous training was thought necessary; or, at most, he
was sent to make a short trip in a man-of-war, where he
was subjected to no discipline, where he was treated with
marked respect, and where he lived in a round of revels and
20 amusements. If, in the intervals of feasting, drinking, and
gambling, he succeeded in learning the meaning of a few
technical phrases and the names of the points of the compass, he was fully qualified to take charge of a three-decker.
This is no imaginary description. In 1666, John Sheffield,
25 Earl of Mulgrave, at seventeen years of age, volunteered to
serve at sea against the Dutch. He passed six weeks on
board, diverting himself, as well as he could, in the society
of some young libertines of rank, and then returned home
to take the command of a troop of horse. After this he was
30 never on the water till the year 1672, when he again joined
the fleet, and was almost immediately appointed captain of
a ship of eighty-four guns, reputed the finest in the navy.
He was then twenty-three years old, and had not, in the
whole course of his life, been three months afloat. As soon

as he came back from sea he was made colonel of a regiment of foot.   This is a specimen of the manner in which naval commands of the highest importance were then given, and a favorable specimen ; for Mulgrave, though he wanted experience, wanted neither parts nor courage.   Others were 5 promoted in the same way who not only were not good officers, but who were intellectually and morally incapable of ever becoming good officers, and whose only recommendation was that they had been ruined by folly and vice. The chief bait which allured these men into the service was 10 the profit of conveying bullion and other valuable commodities from port to port, for both the Atlantic and the Mediterranean were then so much infested by pirates from Barbary that merchants were not willing to trust precious cargoes to any custody but that of a man-of-war.   A captain 15 in this way sometimes cleared several thousands of pounds by a short voyage, and for this lucrative business he too often neglected the interests of his country and the honor of his flag, made mean submissions to foreign powers, disobeyed the most direct injunctions of his superiors, lay in port when 20 he was ordered to chase a Sallee rover, or ran with dollars to Leghorn when his instructions directed him to repair to Lisbon.   And all this he did with impunity.   The same interest which had placed him in a post for which he was unfit maintained him there.   No admiral, bearded by these 25 corrupt and dissolute minions of the palace, dared to do more than mutter something about a court-martial.   If any officer showed a higher sense of duty than his fellows, he soon found that he lost money without acquiring honor. One captain who, by strictly obeying the orders of the 30 admiralty, missed a cargo which would have been worth four thousand pounds to him was told by Charles, with ignoble levity, that he was a great fool for his pains.

The discipline of the navy was of a piece throughout.

As the courtly captain despised the admiralty, he was in
turn despised by his crew.   It could not be concealed that
he was inferior in seamanship to every foremast man on
board.   It was idle to expect that old sailors, familiar with
5 the hurricanes of the tropics and with the icebergs of the
Arctic Circle, would pay prompt and respectful obedience to
a chief who knew no more of winds and waves than could
be learned in a gilded barge between Whitehall Stairs [88] and
Hampton Court.[89]   To trust such a novice with the working
10 of a ship was evidently impossible.   The direction of the
navigation was therefore taken from the captain and given
to the master; but this partition of authority produced
innumerable inconveniences.   The line of demarcation was
not, and perhaps could not be, drawn with precision.   There
15 was, therefore, constant wrangling.   The captain, confident
in proportion to his ignorance, treated the master with lordly
contempt.   The master, well aware of the danger of dis-
obliging the powerful, too often, after a struggle, yielded
against his better judgment; and it was well if the loss of
20 ship and crew was not the consequence.   In general, the
least mischievous of the aristocratic captains were those who
completely abandoned to others the direction of their vessels,
and thought only of making money and spending it.   The
way in which these men lived was so ostentatious and volup-
25 tuous that, greedy as they were of gain, they seldom became
rich.   They dressed as if for a gala at Versailles, ate off
plate, drank the richest wines, and kept harems on board,
while hunger and scurvy raged among the crews, and while
corpses were daily flung out of the port-holes.
30   Such was the ordinary character of those who were then
called gentlemen captains.   Mingled with them were to be
found, happily for our country, naval commanders of a very
different description, men whose whole life had been passed
on the deep, and who had worked and fought their way from

the lowest offices of the forecastle to rank and distinction. One of the most eminent of these officers was Sir Christopher Mings, who entered the service as a cabin boy, who fell fighting bravely against the Dutch, and whom his crew, weeping and vowing vengeance, carried to the grave. From him sprang, by a singular kind of descent, a line of valiant and expert sailors. His cabin boy was Sir John Narborough; and the cabin boy of Sir John Narborough was Sir Cloudesley Shovel.[40] To the strong natural sense and dauntless courage of this class of men England owes a debt never to be forgotten. It was by such resolute hearts that, in spite of much maladministration, and in spite of the blunders of more courtly admirals, our coasts were protected and the reputation of our flag upheld during many gloomy and perilous years. But to a landsman these tarpaulins, as they were called, seemed a strange and half-savage race. All their knowledge was professional; and their professional knowledge was practical rather than scientific. Off their own element they were as simple as children. Their deportment was uncouth. There was roughness in their very good-nature; and their talk, where it was not made up of nautical phrases, was too commonly made up of oaths and curses. Such were the chiefs in whose rude school were formed those sturdy warriors from whom Smollett,[41] in the next age, drew Lieutenant Bowling and Commodore Trunnion. But it does not appear that there was in the service of any of the Stuarts a single naval officer such as, according to the notions of our times, a naval officer ought to be, that is to say, a man versed in the theory and practice of his calling, and steeled against all the dangers of battle and tempest, yet of cultivated mind and polished manners. There were gentlemen and there were seamen in the navy of Charles the Second. But the seamen were not gentlemen, and the gentlemen were **not seamen.**

The English navy at that time might, according to the most exact estimates which have come down to us, have been kept in an efficient state for three hundred and eighty thousand pounds a year. Four hundred thousand pounds a year
5 was the sum actually expended, but expended, as we have seen, to very little purpose. The cost of the French marine was nearly the same; the cost of the Dutch marine considerably more.

The charge of the English ordnance in the seventeenth
10 century was, as compared with other military and naval charges, much smaller than at present. At most of the garrisons there were gunners, and here and there, at an important post, an engineer was to be found. But there was no regiment of artillery, no brigade of sappers and miners, no col-
15 lege in which young soldiers could learn the scientific part of war. The difficulty of moving field-pieces was extreme. When, a few years later, William marched from Devonshire to London, the apparatus which he brought with him, though such as had long been in constant use on the Continent, and
20 such as would now be regarded at Woolwich as rude and cumbrous, excited in our ancestors an admiration resembling that which the Indians of America felt for the Castilian arquebusses. The stock of gunpowder kept in the English forts and arsenals was boastfully mentioned by patriotic
25 writers as something which might well impress neighboring nations with awe. It amounted to fourteen or fifteen thousand barrels, about a twelfth of the quantity which it is now thought necessary to have always in store. The expenditure under the head of Ordnance was on an average a little above
30 sixty thousand pounds a year.

The whole effective charge of the army, navy, and ordnance was about seven hundred and fifty thousand pounds. The non-effective charge, which is now a heavy part of our public burdens, can hardly be said to have existed. A very

small number of naval officers, who were not employed in
the public service, drew half pay. No lieutenant was on the
list, nor any captain who had not commanded a ship of the
first or second rate. As the country then possessed only
seventeen ships of the first and second rates that had ever 5
been at sea, and as a large proportion of the persons who
had commanded such ships had good posts on shore, the
expenditure under this head must have been small indeed.
In the army, half pay was given merely as a special and temporary allowance to a small number of officers belonging to 10
two regiments, which were peculiarly situated. Greenwich
Hospital had not been founded. Chelsea Hospital was
building; but the cost of that institution was defrayed partly
by a deduction from the pay of the troops, and partly by private subscription. The king promised to contribute only 15
twenty thousand pounds for architectural expenses, and five
thousand a year for the maintenance of the invalids. It was
no part of the plan that there should be outpensioners. The
whole non-effective charge, military and naval, can scarcely
have exceeded ten thousand pounds a year. It now exceeds 20
ten thousand pounds a day.

Of the expense of civil government only a small portion
was defrayed by the crown. The great majority of the
functionaries whose business was to administer justice and
preserve order either gave their services to the public gratui- 25
tously, or were remunerated in a manner which caused no
drain on the revenue of the state. The sheriffs, mayors, and
aldermen of the towns, the country gentlemen who were in
the commission of the peace, the headboroughs, bailiffs, and
petty constables, cost the king nothing. The superior courts 30
of law were chiefly supported by fees.

Our relations with foreign courts had been put on the
most economical footing. The only diplomatic agent who
had the title of ambassador resided at Constantinople, and

was partly supported by the Turkey Company. Even at the
court of Versailles England had only an envoy; and she had
not even an envoy at the Spanish, Swedish, and Danish
courts. The whole expense under this head cannot, in the
5 last year of the reign of Charles the Second, have much
exceeded twenty thousand pounds.

In this frugality there was nothing laudable. Charles was,
as usual, niggardly in the wrong place, and munificent in the
wrong place. The public service was starved that courtiers
10 might be pampered. The expense of the navy, of the ordnance, of pensions to needy old officers, of missions to foreign
courts, must seem small indeed to the present generation.
But the personal favorites of the sovereign, his ministers, and
the creatures of those ministers, were gorged with public
15 money. Their salaries and pensions, when compared with
the incomes of the nobility, the gentry, the commercial and
professional men of that age, will appear enormous. The
greatest estates in the kingdom then very little exceeded
twenty thousand a year. The Duke of Ormond had twenty-
20 two thousand a year. The Duke of Buckingham, before his
extravagance had impaired his great property, had nineteen
thousand six hundred a year. George Monk, Duke of Albemarle, who had been rewarded for his eminent services with
immense grants of crown land, and who had been notorious
25 both for covetousness and for parsimony, left fifteen thousand
a year of real estate, and sixty thousand pounds in money
which probably yielded seven per cent. These three dukes
were supposed to be three of the very richest subjects
in England. The archbishop of Canterbury can hardly have
30 had five thousand a year. The average income of a temporal peer was estimated, by the best-informed persons, at
about three thousand a year, the average income of a baronet
at nine hundred a year, the average income of a member of
parliament at less than eight hundred a year. A thousand

a year was thought a large revenue for a barrister. Two thousand a year was hardly to be made in the Court of King's Bench, except by the crown lawyers. It is evident, therefore, that an official man would have been well paid if he had received a fourth or fifth part of what would now be 5 an adequate stipend. In fact, however, the stipends of the higher class of official men were as large as at present, and not seldom larger. The lord treasurer, for example, had eight thousand a year, and, when the treasury was in commission, the junior lords had sixteen hundred a year each. 10 The paymaster of the forces had a poundage,[42] amounting to about five thousand a year, on all the money which passed through his hands. The groom of the stole[43] had five thousand a year, the commissioners of the customs twelve hundred a year each, the lords of the bedchamber a thousand a year 15 each. The regular salary, however, was the smallest part of the gains of an official man of that age. From the noblemen who held the white staff and the great seal down to the humblest tidewaiter and gauger, what would now be called gross corruption was practiced without disguise and without 20 reproach. Titles, places, commissions, pardons were daily sold in market overt by the great dignitaries of the realm; and every clerk in every department imitated, to the best of his power, the evil example.

During the last century no prime minister, however pow- 25 erful, has become rich in office, and several prime ministers have impaired their private fortune in sustaining their public character. In the seventeenth century a statesman who was at the head of affairs might easily, and without giving scandal, accumulate in no long time an estate amply sufficient to 30 support a dukedom. It is probable that the income of the prime minister, during his tenure of power, far exceeded that of any other subject. The place of lord lieutenant of Ireland was supposed to be worth forty thousand pounds a

year. The gains of the Chancellor Clarendon, of Arlington,
of Lauderdale, and of Danby were enormous. The sumptuous palace to which the populace of London gave the
name of Dunkirk House, the stately pavilions, the fish ponds,
5 the deer park, and the orangery of Euston, the more than
Italian luxury of Ham, with its busts, fountains, and aviaries,
were among the many signs which indicated what was the
shortest road to boundless wealth. This is the true explanation of the unscrupulous violence with which the statesmen
10 of that day struggled for office, of the tenacity with which,
in spite of vexations, humiliations, and dangers, they clung
to it, and of the scandalous compliances to which they
stooped in order to retain it. Even in our own age, great
as is the power of opinion, and high as is the standard of
15 integrity, there would be great risk of a lamentable change
in the character of our public men, if the place of first lord
of the treasury or secretary of state were worth a hundred
thousand pounds a year. Happily for our country the
emoluments of the highest class of functionaries have not
20 only not grown in proportion to the general growth of our
opulence, but have positively diminished.

The fact that the sum raised in England by taxation has
in a time not exceeding two long lives been mutiplied thirty-
fold is strange, and may at first sight seem appalling. But
25 those who are alarmed by the increase of the public burdens
may perhaps be reassured when they have considered the
increase of the public resources. In the year 1685 the value
of the produce of the soil far exceeded the value of all the
other fruits of human industry. Yet agriculture was in what
30 would now be considered as a very rude and imperfect state.
The arable land and pasture land were not supposed by the
best political arithmeticians of that age to amount to much
more than half the area of the kingdom. The remainder
was believed to consist of moor, forest, and fen. These

computations are strongly confirmed by the road books and
maps of the seventeenth century.　From those books and
maps it is clear that many routes which now pass through an
endless succession of orchards, hayfields, and beanfields then
ran through nothing but heath, swamp, and warren.*　In 5
the drawings of English landscapes made in that age for the
Grand Duke Cosmo, scarce a hedgerow is to be seen, and
numerous tracts, now rich with cultivation, appear as bare
as Salisbury Plain.[44]　At Enfield, hardly out of sight of the
smoke of the capital, was a region of five and twenty miles 10
in circumference which contained only three houses and
scarcely any enclosed fields.　Deer, as free as in an American
forest, wandered there by thousands.[45]　It is to be remarked
that wild animals of large size were then far more numerous
than at present.　The last wild boars, indeed, which had 15
been preserved for the royal diversion, and had been allowed
to ravage the cultivated land with their tusks, had been
slaughtered by the exasperated rustics during the license of
the Civil War.　The last wolf that has roamed our island had
been slain in Scotland a short time before the close of the 20
reign of Charles the Second.　But many breeds, now extinct
or rare, both of quadrupeds and birds, were still common.
The fox, whose life is, in many counties, held almost as
sacred as that of a human being, was considered as a mere
nuisance.　Oliver St. John told the Long Parliament that 25
Strafford was to be regarded, not as a stag or a hare, to whom
some law was to be given, but as a fox, who was to be snared
by any means, and knocked on the head without pity.　This
illustration would be by no means a happy one if addressed
to country gentlemen of our time; but in St. John's day 30

---

* The proportion of unenclosed country seems to have been very
great.　From Abingdon to Gloucester, for example, a distance of forty
or fifty miles, there was not a single enclosure, and scarcely one enclosure between Biggleswade and Lincoln.

there were not seldom great massacres of foxes to which the
peasantry thronged with all the dogs that could be mustered;
traps were set; nets were spread; no quarter was given ; and
to shoot a female with cub was considered as a feat which
5 merited the gratitude of the neighborhood.   The red deer
were then as common in Gloucestershire and Hampshire as
they now are among the Grampian Hills.   On one occasion
Queen Anne,[46] on her way to Portsmouth, saw a herd of no
less than five hundred.   The wild bull with his white mane
10 was still to be found wandering in a few of the southern
forests.   The badger made his dark and tortuous hole on the
side of every hill where the copsewood grew thick.   The
wild cats were frequently heard by night wailing round
the lodges of the rangers of Whittlebury and Needwood.
15 The yellow-breasted martin was still pursued in Cranbourne
Chase for his fur, reputed inferior only to that of the sable.
Fen eagles, measuring more than nine feet between the
extremities of the wings, preyed on fish along the coast of
Norfolk.   On all the downs, from the British Channel to
20 Yorkshire, huge bustards strayed in troops of fifty or sixty,
and were often hunted with greyhounds.   The marshes of
Cambridgeshire and Lincolnshire were covered during some
months of every year by immense clouds of cranes.   Some
of these races the progress of cultivation has extirpated.
25 Of others the numbers are so much diminished that men
crowd to gaze at a specimen as at a Bengal tiger or a Polar
bear.

The progress of this great change can nowhere be more
clearly traced than in the Statute Book.   The number of
30 enclosure acts passed since King George the Second came
to the throne exceeds four thousand.[47]   The area enclosed
under the authority of those acts exceeds, on a moderate
calculation, ten thousand square miles.   How many square
miles which formerly lay waste have, during the same period,

been fenced and carefully tilled by the proprietors, without any application to the legislature, can only be conjectured. But it seems highly probable that a fourth part of England has been, in the course of little more than a century, turned from a wild into a garden.   5

Even in those parts of the kingdom which at the close of the reign of Charles the Second were the best cultivated, the farming, though greatly improved since the Civil War, was not such as would now be thought skillful.   To this day no effectual steps have been taken by public authority for the   10 purpose of obtaining accurate accounts of the produce of the English soil.   The historian must therefore follow, with some misgivings, the guidance of those writers on statistics whose reputation for diligence and fidelity stands highest. At present an average crop of wheat, rye, barley, oats, and   15 beans is supposed considerably to exceed thirty millions of quarters.   The crop of wheat would be thought poor if it did not exceed twelve millions of quarters.   According to the computation made in the year 1696 by Gregory King, the whole quantity of wheat, rye, barley, oats, and   20 beans then annually grown in the kingdom was somewhat less than ten millions of quarters.   The wheat, which was then cultivated only on the strongest clay and consumed only by those who were in easy circumstances, he estimated at less than two millions of quarters.   Charles Davenant, an   25 acute and well-informed, though most unprincipled and rancorous, politician, differed from King as to some of the items of the account, but came to nearly the same general conclusions.

The rotation of crops was very imperfectly understood.   30 It was known, indeed, that some vegetables lately introduced into our island, particularly the turnip, afforded excellent nutriment in winter to sheep and oxen ; but it was not yet the practice to feed cattle in this manner.   It was therefore

by no means easy to keep them alive during the season when
the grass is scanty.   They were killed in great numbers and
salted at the beginning of the cold weather; and, during several months, even the gentry tasted scarcely any fresh animal
5 food, except game and river fish, which were consequently
much more important articles in housekeeping than at present.   It appears from the *Northumberland Household Book* [48]
that, in the reign of Henry the Seventh, fresh meat was
never eaten even by the gentlemen attendant on a great earl,
10 except during the short interval between midsummer and
Michaelmas.   But in the course of two centuries an improvement had taken place ; and under Charles the Second it
was not till the beginning of November that families laid in
their stock of salt provisions, then called Martinmas beef.
15   The sheep and the ox of that time were diminutive when
compared with the sheep and oxen which are now driven to
our markets.   Our native horses, though serviceable, were
held in small esteem and fetched low prices.   They were
valued, one with another, by the ablest of those who computed
20 the national wealth, at not more than fifty shillings each.
Foreign breeds were greatly preferred.   Spanish jennets
were regarded as the finest chargers, and were imported for
purposes of pageantry and war.   The coaches of the aristocracy were drawn by gray Flemish mares, which trotted,
25 as it was thought, with a peculiar grace, and endured better
than any cattle reared in our island the work of dragging a
ponderous equipage over the rugged pavement of London.
Neither the modern dray horse nor the modern race horse
was then known.   At a much later period the ancestors of
30 the gigantic quadrupeds, which all foreigners now class
among the chief wonders of London, were brought from the
marshes of Walcheren; the ancestors of Childers and Eclipse
from the sands of Arabia.   Already, however, there was
among our nobility and gentry a passion for the amusements

of the turf. The importance of improving our studs by an infusion of new blood was strongly felt; and with this view a considerable number of barbs had lately been brought into the country. Two men whose authority on such subjects was held in great esteem, the Duke of Newcastle and Sir John Fenwick, pronounced that the meanest hack ever imported from Tangier would produce a finer progeny than could be expected from the best sire of our native breed. They would not readily have believed that a time would come when the princes and nobles of neighboring lands would be as eager to obtain horses from England as ever the English had been to obtain horses from Barbary.*

The increase of vegetable and animal produce, though great, seems small when compared with the increase of our mineral wealth. In 1685 the tin of Cornwall, which had, more than two thousand years before, attracted the Tyrian sails beyond the pillars of Hercules,[49] was still one of the most valuable subterranean productions of the island. The quantity annually extracted from the earth was found to be, some years later, sixteen hundred tons, probably about a third of what it now is. But the veins of copper which lie in the same region were, in the time of Charles the Second, altogether neglected, nor did any land-owner take them into the account in estimating the value of his property. Cornwall and Wales at present yield annually near fifteen thousand tons of copper, worth near a million and a half sterling, that is to say, worth about twice as much as the annual produce of all English mines of all descriptions in the seventeenth century. The first bed of rock salt had been discovered not long after the Restoration in Cheshire, but does

* The "dappled Flanders mares" were marks of greatness in the time of Pope, and even later. The vulgar proverb that the gray mare is the better horse originated, I suspect, in the preference generally given to the gray mares of Flanders over the finest coach horses of England.

not appear to have been worked in that age.   The salt,
which was obtained by a rude process from brine pits, was
held in no high estimation.   The pans in which the manufacture was carried on exhaled a sulphurous stench ; and,
5 when the evaporation was complete, the substance which was
left was scarcely fit to be used with food.   Physicians attributed the scorbutic and pulmonary complaints which were
common among the English to this unwholesome condiment.
It was therefore seldom used by the upper and middle
10 classes ; and there was a regular and considerable importa-
tion from France.   At present our springs and mines not
only supply our own immense demand, but send annually
seven hundred millions of pounds of excellent salt to foreign
countries.
15   Far more important has been the improvement of our iron
works.   Such works had long existed in our island, but had
not prospered, and had been regarded with no favorable eye
by the government and by the public.   It was not then the
practice to employ coal for smelting the ore ; and the rapid
20 consumption of wood excited the alarm of politicians.   As
early as the reign of Elizabeth there had been loud complaints that whole forests were cut down for the purpose of
feeding the furnaces ; and the parliament had interfered to
prohibit the manufacturers from burning timber.   The manu-
25 facture consequently languished.   At the close of the reign
of Charles the Second, great part of the iron which was
used in the country was imported from abroad; and the whole
quantity cast here annually seems not to have exceeded ten
thousand tons.   At present the trade is thought to be in a
30 depressed state if less than eight hundred thousand tons are
produced in a year.
  One mineral, perhaps more important than iron itself,
remains to be mentioned.   Coal, though very little used in
any species of manufacture, was already the ordinary fuel

in some districts which were fortunate enough to possess
large beds, and in the capital, which could easily be supplied
by water carriage.   It seems reasonable to believe that at
least one-half of the quantity then extracted from the pits
was consumed in London.   The consumption of London   5
seemed to the writers of that age enormous, and was often
mentioned by them as a proof of the greatness of the imperial city.   They scarcely hoped to be believed when they
affirmed that two hundred and eighty thousand chaldrons,
that is to say, about three hundred and fifty thousand tons, 10
were, in the last year of the reign of Charles the Second,
brought to the Thames.   At present near three millions and
a half of tons are required yearly by the metropolis; and the
whole annual produce cannot, on the most moderate computation, be estimated at less than twenty millions of tons.*   15
   While these great changes have been in progress, the rent
of land has, as might be expected, been almost constantly
rising.   In some districts it has multiplied more than tenfold.
In some it has not more than doubled.   It has probably, on
the average, quadrupled.   20
   Of the rent, a large proportion was divided among the
country gentlemen, a class of persons whose position and
character it is most important that we should clearly understand ; for by their influence and by their passions the
fate of the nation was, at several important conjunctures, 25
determined.
   We should be much mistaken if we pictured to ourselves
the squires of the seventeenth century as men bearing a close
resemblance to their descendants, the county members and
chairmen of quarter sessions with whom we are familiar. 30
The modern country gentleman generally receives a liberal
education, passes from a distinguished school to a distin-

* In 1845 the quantity of coal brought into London appeared, by the
parliamentary returns, to be 3,460,000 tons.

guished college, and has every opportunity to become an
excellent scholar.   He has generally seen something of foreign countries.   A considerable part of his life has generally
been passed in the capital, and the refinements of the capital
5 follow him into the country.   There is perhaps no class of
dwellings so pleasing as the rural seats of the English gentry.
In the parks and pleasure-grounds, nature, dressed yet not
disguised by art, wears her almost alluring form.   In the
buildings good sense and good taste combine to produce a
10 happy union of the comfortable and the graceful.   The pictures, the musical instruments, the library would in any
other country be considerered as proving the owner to be
an eminently polished and accomplished man.   A country
gentleman who witnessed the Revolution was probably in
15 receipt of about a fourth part of the rent which his acres
now yield to his posterity.   He was, therefore, as compared
with his posterity, a poor man, and was generally under the
necessity of residing, with little interruption, on his estate.
To travel on the Continent, to maintain an establishment in
20 London, or even to visit London frequently, were pleasures
in which only the great proprietors could indulge.   It may
be confidently affirmed that of the squires whose names were
in King Charles's commissions of peace and lieutenancy not
one in twenty went to town once in five years, or had ever
25 in his life wandered so far as Paris.   Many lords of manors
had received an education differing little from that of their
menial servants.   The heir of an estate often passed his
boyhood and youth at the seat of his family with no better
tutors than grooms and gamekeepers, and scarce attained
30 learning enough to sign his name to a mittimus.   If he went
to school and to college, he generally returned before he was
twenty to the seclusion of the old hall, and there, unless his
mind were very happily constituted by nature, soon forgot
his academical pursuits in rural business and pleasures.

His chief serious employment was the care of his property. He examined samples of grain, handled pigs, and on market days made bargains over a tankard with drovers and hop merchants. His chief pleasures were commonly derived from field sports and from an unrefined sensuality. His language and pronunciation were such as we should now expect to hear only from the most ignorant clowns. His oaths, coarse jests, and scurrilous terms of abuse were uttered with the broadest accent of his province. It was easy to discern, from the first words which he spoke, whether he came from Somersetshire or Yorkshire. He troubled himself little about decorating his abode, and, if he attempted decoration, seldom produced anything but deformity. The litter of a farmyard gathered under the windows of his bedchamber, and the cabbages and gooseberry bushes grew close to his hall door. His table was loaded with coarse plenty, and guests were cordially welcomed to it. But, as the habit of drinking to excess was general in the class to which he belonged, and as his fortune did not enable him to intoxicate large assemblies daily with claret or canary, strong beer was the ordinary beverage. The quantity of beer consumed in those days was indeed enormous. For beer then was to the middle and lower classes, not only all that beer now is, but all that wine, tea, and ardent spirits now are. It was only at great houses or on great occasions that foreign drink was placed on the board. The ladies of the house, whose business it had commonly been to cook the repast, retired as soon as the dishes had been devoured, and left the gentlemen to their ale and tobacco. The coarse jollity of the afternoon was often prolonged till the revellers were laid under the table.

It was very seldom that the country gentleman caught glimpses of the great world, and what he saw of it tended rather to confuse than to enlighten his understanding. His opinions respecting religion, government, foreign countries,

and former times, having been derived, not from study, from
observation, or from conversation with enlightened companions, but from such traditions as were current in his own
small circle, were the opinions of a child.   He adhered to
5 them, however, with the obstinacy which is generally found
in ignorant men accustomed to be fed with flattery.   His
animosities were numerous and bitter.   He hated French-
men and Italians, Scotchmen and Irishmen, Papists and
Presbyterians, Independents and Baptists, Quakers and
10 Jews.   Towards London and Londoners he felt an aversion
which more than once produced important political effects.
His wife and daughter were in tastes and acquirements
below a housekeeper or a stillroom maid of the present day.
They stitched and spun, brewed gooseberry wine, cured
15 marigolds, and made the crust for the venison pasty.

From this description it might be supposed that the English esquire of the seventeenth century did not materially
differ from a rustic miller or alehouse keeper of our time.
There are, however, some important parts of his character
20 still to be noted which will greatly modify this estimate.
Unlettered as he was and unpolished, he was still in some
most important points a gentleman.   He was a member of
a proud and powerful aristocracy, and was distinguished by
many both of the good and of the bad qualities which belong
25 to aristocrats.   His family pride was beyond that of a
Talbot or a Howard.   He knew the genealogies and coats-
of-arms of all his neighbors, and could tell which of them
had assumed supporters without any right, and which of
them were so unfortunate as to be great-grandsons of alder-
30 men.   He was a magistrate, and, as such, administered
gratuitously to those who dwelt around him a rude patri-
archal justice, which, in spite of innumerable blunders and
of occasional acts of tyranny, was yet better than no justice
at all.   He was an officer of the trainbands, and his military

dignity, though it might move the mirth of gallants who had served a campaign in Flanders, raised his character in his own eyes and in the eyes of his neighbors. Nor indeed was his soldiership justly a subject of derision. In every county there were elderly gentlemen who had seen service 5 which was no child's play. One had been knighted by Charles the First after the battle of Edgehill. Another still wore a patch over the scar which he had received at Naseby. A third had defended his old house till Fairfax had blown in the door with a petard. The presence of these old Cava- 10 liers with their old swords and holsters, and with their old stories about Goring and Lunsford, gave to the musters of militia an earnest and warlike aspect which would otherwise have been wanting. Even those country gentlemen who were too young to have themselves exchanged blows with 15 the cuirassiers of the parliament had, from childhood, been surrounded by the traces of recent war and fed with stories of the martial exploits of their fathers and uncles. Thus the character of the English esquire of the seventeenth century was compounded of two elements which we are not accus- 20 tomed to find united. His ignorance and uncouthness, his low tastes and gross phrases would, in our time, be considered as indicating a nature and a breeding thoroughly plebeian. Yet he was essentially a patrician, and had, in large measure, both the virtues and the vices which flourish 25 among men set from their birth in high place, and accustomed to authority, to observance, and to self-respect. It is not easy for a generation which is accustomed to find chivalrous sentiments only in company with liberal studies and polished manners to imagine to itself a man with the 30 deportment, the vocabulary, and the accent of a carter, yet punctilious on matters of genealogy and precedence, and ready to risk his life rather than see a stain cast on the honor of his house. It is only, however, by thus joining

together things seldom or never found together in our own experience that we can form a just idea of that rustic aristocracy which constituted the main strength of the armies of Charles the First, and which long supported, with strange
5 fidelity, the interest of his descendants.

The gross, uneducated, untraveled country gentleman was commonly a Tory, but, though devotedly attached to hereditary monarchy, he had no partiality for courtiers and ministers. He thought, not without reason, that Whitehall was
10 filled with the most corrupt of mankind; that of the great sums which the House of Commons had voted to the crown since the Restoration part had been embezzled by cunning politicians and part squandered on buffoons and foreign courtesans. His stout English heart swelled with indigna-
15 tion at the thought that the government of his country should be subject to French dictation. Being himself generally an old Cavalier or the son of an old Cavalier, he reflected with bitter resentment on the ingratitude with which the Stuarts had requited their best friends. Those who
20 heard him grumble at the neglect with which he was treated, and at the profusion with which wealth was lavished on the bastards of Nell Gwynn and Madam Carwell,[50] would have supposed him ripe for rebellion. But all this ill humor lasted only till the throne was really in danger. It was pre-
25 cisely when those whom the sovereign had loaded with wealth and honors shrank from his side that the country gentlemen, so surly and mutinous in the season of his prosperity, rallied round him in a body. Thus, after murmuring twenty years at the misgovernment of Charles the Second,
30 they came to his rescue in his extremity when his own secretaries of state and lords of the treasury had deserted him, and enabled him to gain a complete victory over the opposition; nor can there be any doubt that they would have shown equal loyalty to his brother James, if James

would, even at the moment, have refrained from outraging their strongest feeling. For there was one institution, and one only, which they prized even more then hereditary monarchy, and that institution was the Church of England. Their love of the Church was not, indeed, the effect of study or meditation. Few among them could have given any reason, drawn from Scripture or ecclesiastical history, for adhering to her doctrines, her ritual, and her polity; nor were they, as a class, by any means strict observers of that code of morality which is common to all Christian sects. But the experience of many ages proves that men may be ready to fight to the death, and to persecute without pity, for a religion whose creed they do not understand and whose precepts they habitually disobey.

The rural clergy were even more vehement in Toryism than the rural gentry, and were a class scarcely less important. It is to be observed, however, that the individual clergyman, as compared with the individual gentleman, then ranked much lower than in these days. The main support of the Church was derived from the tithe; and the tithe bore to the rent a much smaller ratio than at present. King estimated the whole income of the parochial and collegiate clergy at only four hundred and eighty thousand pounds a year; Davenant at only five hundred and forty-four thousand a year. It is certainly now more than seven times as great as the larger of these two sums. It follows that rectors and vicars must have been, as compared with the neighboring knights and squires, much poorer in the seventeenth than in the nineteenth century.

The place of the clergyman in society had been completely changed by the Reformation. Before that event, ecclesiastics had formed the majority of the House of Lords, had, in wealth and splendor, equaled, and sometimes outshone, the greatest of the temporal barons, and had generally held

the highest civil offices. The lord treasurer was often a
bishop. The lord chancellor was almost always so. The
lord keeper of the privy seal and the master of the rolls
were ordinarily churchmen. Churchmen transacted the
5 most important diplomatic business. Indeed, almost all
that large portion of the administration which rude and warlike nobles were incompetent to conduct was considered as
especially belonging to divines. Men, therefore, who were
averse to the life of camps, and who were, at the same time,
10 desirous to rise in the state, ordinarily received the tonsure.
Among them were sons of all the most illustrious families,
and near kinsmen of the throne, Scroops and Nevilles,
Bourchiers, Staffords, and Poles. To the religious houses
belonged the rents of immense domains, and all that large
15 portion of the tithe which is now in the hands of laymen.
Down to the middle of the reign of Henry the Eighth,
therefore, no line of life bore so inviting an aspect to ambitious and covetous natures as the priesthood. Then came
a violent revolution. The abolition of the monasteries
20 deprived the Church at once of the greater part of her
wealth, and of her predominance in the Upper House of
parliament. There was no longer an abbot of Glastonbury[51] or an abbot of Reading[52] seated among the peers,
and possessed of revenues equal to those of a powerful earl.
25 The princely splendor of William of Wykeham[53] and of
William of Waynflete[54] had disappeared. The scarlet hat
of the cardinal, the silver cross of the legate were no more.
The clergy had also lost the ascendency which is the natural
reward of superior mental cultivation. Once the circum-
30 stance that a man could read had raised a presumption that
he was in orders. But in an age which produced such laymen as William Cecil and Nicholas Bacon, Roger Ascham
and Thomas Smith, Walter Mildmay and Francis Walsingham,[55] there was no reason for calling away prelates

from their dioceses to negotiate treaties, to superintend the
finances, or to administer justice.   The spiritual character
not only ceased to be a qualification for high civil office, but
began to be regarded as a disqualification.   Those worldly
motives, therefore, which had formerly induced so many   5
able, aspiring, and high-born youths to assume the ecclesiastical habit ceased to exist.   Not one parish in two hundred
then afforded what a man of family considered as a maintenance.   There were still indeed prizes in the Church, but they
were few; and even the highest were mean, when compared   10
with the glory which had once surrounded the princes of the
hierarchy.   The state kept by Parker and Grindal [56] seemed
beggarly to those who remembered the imperial pomp of
Wolsey,[57] his palaces, which had become the favorite abodes
of royalty, Whitehall and Hampton Court, the three sumptu-   15
ous tables daily spread in his hall, the forty-four gorgeous
copes in his chapel, his running footmen in rich liveries, and
his body-guards with gilded pole axes.   Thus the sacerdotal
office lost its attraction for the higher classes.   During the
century which followed the accession of Elizabeth, scarce   20
a single person of noble descent took orders.   At the close
of the reign of Charles the Second, two sons of peers were
bishops ; four or five sons of peers were priests, and held
valuable preferment; but these rare exceptions did not take
away the reproach which lay on the body.   The clergy were   25
regarded as, on the whole, a plebeian class.   And, indeed,
for one who made the figure of a gentleman, ten were mere
menial servants.   A large proportion of those divines who
had no benefices, or whose benefices were too small to
afford a comfortable revenue, lived in the houses of laymen.   30
It had long been evident that this practice tended to de-
grade the priestly character.   Laud [58] had exerted himself
to effect a change; and Charles the First had repeatedly
issued positive orders that none but men of high rank should

presume to keep domestic chaplains.   But these injunctions
had become obsolete.   Indeed, during the domination of the
Puritans, many of the ejected ministers of the Church of
England could obtain bread and shelter only by attaching
5 themselves to the households of royalist gentlemen ; and the
habits which had been formed in those times of trouble
continued long after the reëstablishment of monarchy and
episcopacy.   In the mansions of men of liberal sentiments
and cultivated understandings, the chaplain was doubtless
10 treated with urbanity and kindness.   His conversation, his
literary assistance, his spiritual advice were considered as an
ample return for his food, his lodging, and his stipend.   But
this was not the general feeling of the country gentlemen.
The coarse and ignorant squire, who thought that it be-
15 longed to his dignity to have grace said every day at his
table by an ecclesiastic in full canonicals, found means to
reconcile dignity with economy.   A young Levite — such
was the phrase then in use — might be had for his board, a
small garret, and ten pounds a year, and might not only
20 perform his own professional functions, might not only be
the most patient of butts and of listeners, might not only
be always ready in fine weather for bowls, and in rainy
weather for shovel-board, but might also save the expense
of a gardener or of a groom.   Sometimes the reverend man
25 nailed up the apricots, and sometimes he curried the coach
horses. He cast up the farrier's bills.   He walked ten
miles with a message or a parcel.   If he was permitted
to dine with the family, he was expected to content himself
with the plainest fare. He might fill himself with the corned
30 beef and the carrots; but as soon as the tarts and cheese-
cakes made their appearance, he quitted his seat, and stood
aloof till he was summoned to return thanks for the repast,
from a great part of which he had been excluded.

Perhaps after some years of service he was presented to a

living sufficient to support him; but he often found it necessary to purchase his preferment by a species of simony,
which furnished an inexhaustible subject of pleasantry to
three or four generations of scoffers. With his cure he was
expected to take a wife. The wife had ordinarily been in ₅
the patron's service; and it was well if she was not suspected
of standing too high in the patron's favor. Indeed, the
nature of the matrimonial connections which the clergymen
of that age were in the habit of forming is the most certain
indication of the place which the order held in the social 1c
system. An Oxonian, writing a few months after the death
of Charles the Second, complained bitterly, not only that
the country attorney and the country apothecary looked
down with disdain on the country clergyman, but that one
of the lessons most earnestly inculcated on every girl of 15
honorable family was to give no encouragement to a lover
in orders, and that, if any young lady forgot this precept,
she was almost as much disgraced as by an illicit amour.
Clarendon,[59] who assuredly bore no ill will to the Church,
mentions it as a sign of the confusion of ranks which the 2c
great rebellion had produced, that some damsels of noble
families had bestowed themselves on divines. A waiting
woman was generally considered as the most suitable help-
mate for a parson. Queen Elizabeth, as head of the Church,
had given what seemed to be a formal sanction to this pre- 25
judice, by issuing special orders that no clergyman should
presume to marry a servant girl without the consent of her
master or mistress. During several generations accordingly
the relation between priests and handmaidens was a theme
for endless jest ; nor would it be easy to find, in the comedy 30
of the seventeenth century, a single instance of a clergyman who wins a spouse above the rank of a cook. Even so
late as the time of George the Second, the keenest of all
observers of life and manners, himself a priest, remarked

that, in a great household, the chaplain was the resource of a lady's maid whose character had been blown upon, and who was therefore forced to give up hopes of catching the steward.[60]

5   In general the divine who quitted his chaplainship for a benefice and a wife found that he had only exchanged one class of vexations for another. Not one living in fifty enabled the incumbent to bring up a family comfortably. As children multiplied and grew, the household of the priest became 10 more and more beggarly. Holes appeared more and more plainly in the thatch of his parsonage and in his single cassock. Often it was only by toiling on his glebe, by feeding swine, and by loading dung-carts that he could obtain daily bread; nor did his utmost exertions always prevent the 15 bailiffs from taking his concordance and his inkstand in execution. It was a white day on which he was admitted into the kitchen of a great house, and regaled by the servants with cold meat and ale. His children were brought up like the children of the neighboring peasantry. 20 His boys followed the plough, and his girls went out to service. Study he found impossible, for the advowson of his living would hardly have sold for a sum sufficient to purchase a good theological library; and he might be considered as unusually lucky if he had ten or 25 twelve dog-eared volumes among the pots and pans on his shelves. Even a keen and strong intellect might be expected to rust in so unfavorable a situation.

Assuredly there was at that time no lack in the English Church of ministers distinguished by abilities and learning. 30 But it is to be observed that these ministers were not scattered among the rural population. They were brought together at a few places where the means of acquiring knowledge were abundant, and where the opportunities of vigorous intellectual exercise were frequent. At such places

were to be found divines qualified by parts, by eloquence,
by wide knowledge of literature, of science, and of life, to
defend their Church victoriously against heretics and scep-
tics, to command the attention of frivolous and worldly con-
gregations, to guide the deliberations of senates, and to make 5
religion respectable, even in the most dissolute of courts.
Some of them labored to fathom the abysses of metaphysical
theology; some were deeply versed in biblical criticism; and
some threw light on the darkest parts of ecclesiastical history. Some proved themselves consummate masters of logic. 10
Some cultivated rhetoric with such assiduity and success that
their discourses are still justly valued as models of style.
These eminent men were to be found, with scarce a single
exception, at the universities, at the great cathedrals, or in
the capital.   Barrow had lately died at Cambridge, and 15
Pearson had gone thence to the episcopal bench. Cudworth
and Henry More were still living there. South and Pococke,
Jane and Aldrich were at Oxford.   Prideaux was in the
close of Norwich, and Whitby in the close of Salisbury. But
it was chiefly by the London clergy, who were always spoken 20
of as a class apart, that the fame of their profession for
learning and eloquence was upheld.   The principal pulpits
of the metropolis were occupied about this time by a crowd
of distinguished men, from among whom was selected a large
proportion of the rulers of the Church.   Sherlock preached 25
at the Temple, Tillotson at Lincoln's Inn, Wake and Jeremy
Collier at Gray's Inn, Burnet at the Rolls, Stillingfleet at
St. Paul's Cathedral, Patrick at St. Paul's, Covent Garden,
Fowler at St. Giles's, Cripplegate, Sharp at St. Giles's in the
Field's, Tennison at St. Martin's, Sprat at St. Margaret's, 30
Beveridge at St. Peter's in Cornhill. Of these twelve men,
all of high note in ecclesiastical history, ten became bishops
and four archbishops. Meanwhile almost the only important
theological works which came forth from a rural parsonage

were those of George Bull, afterwards Bishop of St. David's;
and Bull would never have produced those works had he
not inherited an estate, by the sale of which he was enabled
to collect a library, such as probably no other country clergy-
5 man in England possessed.

Thus the Anglican priesthood was divided into two sec-
tions, which, in acquirements, in manners, and in social
position, differed widely from each other. One section, trained
for cities and courts, comprised men familiar with all ancient
10 and modern learning; men able to encounter Hobbes or
Bossuet [61] at all the weapons of controversy; men who could,
in their sermons, set forth the majesty and beauty of Chris-
tianity with such justness of thought and such energy of
language that the indolent Charles roused himself to listen,
15 and the fastidious Buckingham [62] forgot to sneer; men whose
address, politeness, and knowledge of the world qualified
them to manage the consciences of the wealthy and noble;
men with whom Halifax [63] loved to discuss the interests of
empires, and from whom Dryden was not ashamed to own
20 that he had learned to write.*   The other section was destined to ruder and humbler service. It was dispersed over
the country, and consisted chiefly of persons not at all
wealthier, and not much more refined, than small farmers or
upper servants. Yet it was in these rustic priests, who
25 derived but a scanty subsistence from their tithe sheaves
and tithe pigs, and who had not the smallest chance of ever
attaining high professional honors, that the professional
spirit was strongest. Among those divines who were the
boast of the universities and the delight of the capital, and
30 who had attained, or might reasonably expect to attain,

---

* "I have frequently heard him (Dryden) own with pleasure that, if
he had any talent for English prose, it was owing to his having often
read the writings of the great Archbishop Tillotson." Congreve's
Dedication of Dryden's Plays.

opulence and lordly rank, a party, respectable in numbers, and more respectable in character, leaned towards constitutional principles of government, lived on friendly terms with Presbyterians, Independents, and Baptists, would gladly have seen a full toleration granted to all Protestant sects, and 5 would even have consented to make alterations in the liturgy, for the purpose of conciliating honest and candid Non-conformists. But such latitudinarianism was held in horror by the country parson. He was, indeed, prouder of his ragged gown than his superiors of their lawn and of their scarlet 10 hoods.[64] The very consciousness that there was little in his worldly circumstances to distinguish him from the villagers to whom he preached led him to hold immoderately high the dignity of that sacerdotal office which was his single title to reverence. Having lived in seclusion, and having had little 15 opportunity of correcting his opinions by reading or conversation, he held and taught the doctrines of indefeasible hereditary right, of passive obedience, and of non-resistance, in all their crude absurdity. Having been long engaged in a petty war against the neighboring dissenters, he too often 20 hated them for the wrongs which he had done them, and found no fault with the Five-Mile Act and the Conventicle Act,[65] except that those odious laws had not a sharper edge. Whatever influence his office gave him was exerted with passionate zeal on the Tory side; and that influence was immense. 25 It would be a great error to imagine, because the country rector was in general not regarded as a gentleman, because he could not dare to aspire to the hand of one of the young ladies at the manor house, because he was not asked into the parlors of the great, but was left to drink and smoke with 30 grooms and butlers, that the power of the clerical body was smaller than at present. The influence of a class is by no means proportioned to the consideration which the members of that class enjoy in their individual capacity. A cardinal is a much more exalted personage than a begging friar; but it would be a grievous mistake to suppose that the College of Cardinals has exercised a greater dominion over the public mind of Europe than the order of Saint Francis. 5 In Ireland, at present, a peer holds a far higher station in society than a Roman Catholic priest; yet there are in Munster and Connaught few counties where a combination of priests would not carry an election against a combination of peers. In the seventeenth century the pulpit was to a 10 large portion of the population what the periodical press now is. Scarce any of the clowns who came to the parish church ever saw a gazette or a political pamphlet. Ill informed as their spiritual pastor might be, he was yet better informed than themselves; he had every week an opportunity of 15 haranguing them; and his harangues were never answered. At every important conjuncture, invectives against the Whigs and exhortations to obey the Lord's Anointed resounded at once from many thousands of pulpits; and the effect was for-midable indeed. Of all the causes which, after the dissolution 20 of the Oxford parliament, produced the violent reaction against the Exclusionists,[66] the most potent seems to have been the oratory of the country clergy.

The power which the country gentlemen and the country clergymen exercised in the rural districts was in some meas-25 ure counterbalanced by the power of the yeomanry, an emi-nently manly and true-hearted race. The petty proprietors who cultivated their own fields and enjoyed a modest compe-tence, without affecting to have scutcheons and crests, or aspiring to sit on the bench of justice, then formed a much 30 more important part of the nation than at present. If we may trust the best statistical writers of that age, not less than a hundred and sixty thousand proprietors, who, with their families, must have made up more than a seventh of the whole population, derived their subsistence from little

freehold estates. The average income of these small land-
owners was estimated at between sixty and seventy pounds
a year. It was computed that the number of persons who
occupied their own land was greater than the number of
those who farmed the land of others. A large portion of the 5
yeomanry had, from the time of the Reformation, leaned
towards Puritanism, had, in the Civil War, taken the side
of the parliament, had, after the Restoration, persisted in
hearing Presbyterian and Independent preachers, had, at
elections, strenuously supported the Exclusionists, and had 10
continued, even after the discovery of the Rye House Plot
and the proscription of the Whig leaders, to regard Popery
and arbitrary power with unmitigated hostility.

Great as has been the change in the rural life of England
since the Revolution, the change which has come to pass in 15
the cities is still more amazing. At present a sixth part of
the nation is crowded into provincial towns of more than
thirty thousand inhabitants. In the reign of Charles the
Second no provincial town in the kingdom contained thirty
thousand inhabitants, and only four provincial towns con- 20
tained so many as ten thousand inhabitants.

Next to the capital, but next at an immense distance,
stood Bristol, then the first English seaport, and Norwich,
then the first English manufacturing town. Both have since
that time been far outstripped by younger rivals; yet both 25
have made great positive advances. The population of
Bristol has quadrupled. The population of Norwich has
more than doubled.

Pepys, who visited Bristol eight years after the Restoration, was struck by the splendor of the city. But his stan- 30
dard was not high ; for he noted down as a wonder the
circumstance that, in Bristol, a man might look round him
and see nothing but houses. It seems that, in no other
place with which he was acquainted, except London, did

the buildings completely shut out the woods and fields.
Large as Bristol might then appear, it occupied but a very
small portion of the area on which it now stands. A few
churches of eminent beauty rose out of a labyrinth of
5 narrow lanes built upon vaults of no great solidity. If a
coach or a cart entered these alleys, there was danger that
it would be wedged between the houses, and danger also
that it would break in the cellars. Goods were, therefore,
conveyed about the town almost exclusively in trucks drawn
o by dogs ; and the richest inhabitants exhibited their wealth,
not by riding in gilded carriages, but by walking the streets
with trains of servants in rich liveries, and by keeping
tables loaded with good cheer. The pomp of the christen-
ings and burials far exceeded what was seen at any other
15 place in England. The hospitality of the city was widely
renowned, and especially the collations with which the sugar
refiners regaled their visitors. The repast was dressed in
the furnace, and was accompanied by a rich brewage made
of the best Spanish wine, and celebrated over the whole
20 kingdom as Bristol milk. This luxury was supported by a
thriving trade with the North American plantations and
with the West Indies. The passion for colonial traffic was
so strong that there was scarce a small shopkeeper in
Bristol who had not a venture on board of some ship bound
25 for Virginia or the Antilles. Some of these ventures indeed were not of the most honorable kind. There was, in
the Transatlantic possessions of the crown, a great demand
for labor, and this demand was partly supplied by a system
of crimping and kidnapping at the principal English sea-
30 ports.[67] Nowhere was this system found in such active and
extensive operation as at Bristol. Even the first magistrates
of that city were not ashamed to enrich themselves by so
odious a commerce. The number of houses in the city
appears, from the returns of the hearth money, to have

been, in the year 1685, just five thousand three hundred. We can hardly suppose the number of persons in a house to have been greater than in the city of London; and in the city of London we learn from the best authority that there were then fifty-five persons to ten houses. The population of Bristol must therefore have been twenty-nine thousand souls.

Norwich was the capital of a large and fruitful province. It was the residence of a bishop and of a chapter. It was the chief seat of the chief manufacture of the realm. Some men distinguished by learning and science had recently 10 dwelt there, and no place in the kingdom, except the capital and the universities, had more attractions for the curious. The library, the museum, the aviary, and the botanical garden of Sir Thomas Browne were thought by Fellows of the Royal Society well worthy of a long pilgrimage. 15 Norwich had also a court in miniature. In the heart of the city stood an old palace of the Dukes of Norfolk, said to be the largest town house in the kingdom out of London. In this mansion, to which were annexed a tennis court, a bowling green, and a wilderness stretching along the bank of the 20 Wansum, the noble family of Howard frequently resided, and kept a state resembling that of petty sovereigns. Drink was served to guests in goblets of pure gold. The very tongs and shovels were of silver. Pictures by Italian masters adorned the walls. The cabinets were filled with a 25 fine collection of gems purchased by that Earl of Arundel whose marbles are now among the ornaments of Oxford. Here, in the year 1671, Charles and his court were sumptuously entertained. Here, too, all comers were annually welcomed from Christmas to Twelfth Night. Ale flowed in 30 oceans for the populace. Three coaches, one of which had been built at a cost of five hundred pounds, to contain fourteen persons, were sent every afternoon round the city to bring ladies to the festivities, and the dances were always

followed by a luxurious banquet. When the Duke of Norfolk came to Norwich, he was greeted like a king returning to his capital. The bells of the cathedral and of Saint Peter Mancroft were rung. The guns of the castle were
5 fired, and the mayor and aldermen waited on their illustrious fellow-citizen with complimentary addresses. In the year 1693, the population of Norwich was found by actual enumeration to be between twenty-eight and twenty-nine thousand souls.
10   Far below Norwich, but still high in dignity and importance, were some other ancient capitals of shires. In that age it was seldom that a country gentleman went up with his family to London. The county town was his metropolis. He sometimes made it his residence during part of the
15 year. At all events, he was often attracted thither by business and pleasure, by assizes, quarter sessions, elections, musters of militia, festivals, and races. There were the halls where the judges, robed in scarlet and escorted by javelins and trumpets, opened the king's commission twice
20 a year. There were the markets at which the corn, the cattle, the wool, and the hops of the surrounding country were exposed to sale. There were the great fairs to which merchants came down from London, and where the rural dealer laid in his annual stores of sugar, stationery, cutlery,
25 and muslin. There were the shops at which the best families of the neighborhood bought grocery and millinery. Some of these places derived dignity from interesting historical recollections, from cathedrals decorated by all the art and magnificence of the middle ages, from palaces where
30 a long succession of prelates had dwelt, from closes surrounded by the venerable abodes of deans and canons, and from castles which had in the old time repelled the Nevilles or De Veres, and which bore more recent traces of the vengeance of Rupert or of Cromwell.

Conspicuous among these interesting cities were York, the capital of the north, and Exeter, the capital of the west. Neither can have contained much more than ten thousand inhabitants. Worcester, the queen of the cider land, had about eight thousand; Nottingham probably as many. 5 Gloucester, renowned for that resolute defence which had been fatal to Charles the First, had certainly between four and five thousand; Derby not quite four thousand. Shrewsbury was the chief place of an extensive and fertile district. The court of the marches of Wales was held 10 there. In the language of the gentry many miles round the Wrekin, to go to Shrewsbury was to go to town. The provincial wits and beauties imitated, as well as they could, the fashions of Saint James's Park, in the walks along the side of the Severn. The inhabitants were about seven 15 thousand.

The population of every one of these places has, since the Revolution, much more than doubled. The population of some has multiplied sevenfold. The streets have been almost entirely rebuilt. Slate has succeeded to thatch and 20 brick to timber. The pavements and the lamps, the display of wealth in the principal shops, and the luxurious neatness of the dwellings occupied by the gentry would, in the seventeeth century, have seemed miraculous. Yet is the relative importance of the old capitals of counties by no 25 means what it was. Younger towns, towns which are rarely or never mentioned in our early history, and which sent no representatives to our early parliaments, have, within the memory of persons still living, grown to a greatness which this generation contemplates with wonder and pride, not 30 unaccompanied by awe and anxiety.

The most eminent of these towns were indeed known in the seventeenth century as respectable seats of industry. Nay, their rapid progress and their vast opulence were then

sometimes described in language which seems ludicrous to a
man who has seen their present grandeur.   One of the
most populous and prosperous among them was Manchester.   It had been required by the Protector to send one
5 representative to his parliament, and was mentioned by
writers of the time of Charles the Second as a busy and
opulent place.   Cotton had, during half a century, been
brought thither from Cyprus and Smyrna, but the manufacture was in its infancy.   Whitney [68] had not yet taught how
10 the raw material might be furnished in quantities almost
fabulous.   Arkwright had not yet taught how it might be
worked up with a speed and precision which seem magical.
The whole annual import did not, at the end of the seventeenth century, amount to two millions of pounds, a
15 quantity which would now hardly supply the demand of
forty-eight hours.   That wonderful emporium, which in
population and wealth far surpasses capitals so much .
renowned as Berlin, Madrid, and Lisbon, was then a mean
and ill-built market town, containing under six thousand
20 people.   It then had not a single press.   It now supports a
hundred printing establishments.   It then had not a single
coach.   It now supports twenty coachmakers.

Leeds was already the chief seat of the woolen manufactures of Yorkshire, but the elderly inhabitants could still
25 remember the time when the first brick house, then and
long after called the Red House, was built.   They boasted
loudly of their increasing wealth, and of the immense sales
of cloth which took place in the open air on the bridge.
Hundreds, nay, thousands of pounds had been paid down in
30 the course of one busy market day.   The rising importance
of Leeds had attracted the notice of successive governments.   Charles the First had granted municipal privileges
to the town.   Oliver had invited it to send one member
to the House of Commons.   But from the returns of the

hearth money it seems certain that the whole population of
the borough, an extensive district which contains many hamlets, did not, in the reign of Charles the Second, exceed
seven thousand souls. In 1841 there were more than a
hundred and fifty thousand. 5

About a day's journey south of Leeds, on the verge of a
wild moorland tract, lay an ancient manor, now rich with
cultivation, then barren and unenclosed, which was known
by the name of Hallamshire. Iron abounded there, and
from a very early period, the rude whittles[69] fabricated 10
there had been sold all over the kingdom. They had
indeed been mentioned by Geoffrey Chaucer[70] in one of
his *Canterbury Tales.* But the manufacture appears to
have made little progress during the three centuries which
followed his time. This languor may perhaps be explained 15
by the fact that the trade was, during almost the whole of
this long period, subject to such regulations as the lord and
his court-leet thought fit to impose. The more delicate kinds
of cutlery were either made in the capital or brought from
the Continent. It was not indeed till the reign of George 20
the First that the English surgeons ceased to import from
France those exquisitely fine blades which are required for
operations on the human frame. Most of the Hallamshire
forges were collected in a market town which had sprung
up near the castle of the proprietor, and which, in the reign 25
of James the First, had been a singularly miserable place,
containing about two thousand inhabitants, of whom a third
were half-starved and half-naked beggars. It seems certain
from the parochial registers that the population did not
amount to four thousand at the end of the reign of Charles 30
the Second. The effects of a species of toil singularly unfavorable to the health and vigor of the human frame were
at once discerned by every traveler. A large proportion
of the people had distorted limbs. That is that Sheffield

which now, with its dependencies, contains a hundred and twenty thousand souls, and which sends forth its admirable knives, razors, and lancets to the farthest ends of the world.

5   Birmingham had not been thought of sufficient importance to send a member to Oliver's parliament. Yet the manufacturers of Birmingham were already a busy and thriving race. They boasted that their hardware was highly esteemed, not indeed, as now, at Pekin and Lima, at Bokhara and Timbuc-
10 too, but in London and even as far off as Ireland. They had acquired a less honorable renown as coiners of bad money. In allusion to their spurious groats, the Troy party had fixed on demagogues who hypocritically affected zeal against Popery, the nickname of Birminghams. Yet in 1685 the
15 population, which is now little less than two hundred thousand, did not amount to four thousand. Birmingham buttons were just beginning to be known ; of Birmingham guns nobody had yet heard; and the place whence, two generations later, the magnificent editions of Baskerville went
20 forth to astonish all the librarians of Europe, did not contain a single regular shop where a Bible or an almanac could be bought. On market days a bookseller named Michael Johnson, the father of the great Samuel Johnson,[71] came over from Lichfield, and opened a stall during a few hours.
25 This supply of literature was long found adequate to the demand.

These four chief seats of our great manufactures deserve especial mention. It would be tedious to enumerate all the populous and opulent hives of industry which, a hundred
30 and fifty years ago, were hamlets without a parish church, or desolate moors, inhabited only by grouse and wild deer. Nor has the change been less signal in those outlets by which the products of the English looms and forges are poured forth over the four quarters of the world. At present

Liverpool contains about three hundred thousand inhabitants. The shipping registered at her port amounts to between four and five hundred thousand tons. Into her custom-house has been repeatedly paid in one year a sum more than thrice as great as the whole income of the English crown in 1685. The receipts of her post office, even since the great reduction of the duty, exceed the sum which the postage of the whole kingdom yielded to the Duke of York.[72] Her endless docks and warehouses are among the wonders of the world. Yet even those docks and warehouses seem hardly to suffice for the gigantic trade of the Mersey; and already a rival city is growing fast on the opposite shore. In the days of Charles the Second, Liverpool was described as a rising town which had recently made great advances, and which maintained a profitable intercourse with Ireland and with the sugar colonies. The customs had multiplied eightfold within sixteen years, and amounted to what was then considered the immense sum of fifteen thousand pounds annually. But the population can hardly have exceeded four thousand. The shipping was about fourteen hundred tons, less than the tonnage of a single modern Indiaman of the first class; and the whole number of seamen belonging to the port cannot be estimated at more than two hundred.

Such has been the progress of those towns where wealth is created and accumulated. Not less rapid has been the progress of towns of a very different kind, towns in which wealth, created and accumulated elsewhere, is expended for purposes of health and recreation. Some of the most remarkable of these towns have sprung into existence since the time of the Stuarts. Cheltenham is now a greater city than any which the kingdom contained in the seventeenth century, London alone excepted. But in the seventeenth century, and at the beginning of the eighteenth, Cheltenham

was mentioned by local historians merely as a rural parish
lying under the Cotswold Hills, and affording good ground,
both for tillage and pasture. Corn grew and cattle browsed
over the space now covered by that gay succession of streets
5 and villas. Brighton was described as a place which had
once been thriving, which had possessed many small fishing
barks, and which had, when at the height of prosperity, contained above two thousand inhabitants, but which was sink-
ing fast into decay. The sea was gradually gaining on the
10 buildings, which at length almost entirely disappeared.
Ninety years ago the ruins of an old fort were to be seen
lying among the pebbles and seaweed on the beach; and
ancient men could still point out the traces of foundations
on a spot where a street of more than a hundred huts had
15 been swallowed up by the waves. So desolate was the place
after this calamity that the vicarage was thought scarcely
worth having. A few poor fishermen, however, still continued
to dry their nets on those cliffs, on which now a town more
than twice as large and populous as the Bristol of the Stuarts
20 presents mile after mile its gay and fantastic front to the sea.

England, however, was not, in the seventeenth century,
destitute of watering places. The gentry of Derbyshire and
of the neighboring counties repaired to Buxton, where they
were crowded into low wooden sheds, and regaled with oat-
25 cake, and with a viand which the hosts called mutton, but
which the guests strongly suspected to be dog. Tunbridge
Wells,[73] lying within a day's journey of the capital, and in
one of the richest and most highly civilized parts of the kingdom, had much greater attractions. At present we see there
30 a town which would, a hundred and sixty years ago, have
ranked, in population, fourth or fifth among the towns of
England. The brilliancy of the shops and the luxury of the
private dwellings far surpass anything that England could
then show. When the court, soon after the Restoration,

visited Tunbridge Wells, there was no town there; but, within a mile of the spring, rustic cottages, somewhat cleaner and neater than the ordinary cottages of that time, were scattered over the heath. Some of these cabins were movable, and were carried on sledges from one part of the common to another. To these huts men of fashion, wearied with the din and smoke of London, sometimes came in the summer to breathe fresh air, and to catch a glimpse of rural life. During the season a kind of fair was daily held near the fountain. The wives and daughters of the Kentish farmers came from the neighboring villages with cream, cherries, wheat-ears, and quails. To chaffer with them, to flirt with them, to praise their straw hats and tight heels was a refreshing pastime to voluptuaries sick of the airs of actresses and maids of honor. Milliners, toymen, and jewellers came down from London and opened a bazar under the trees. In one booth the politician might find his coffee and the London *Gazette;* in another were gamblers playing deep at basset[74]; and, on fine evenings, the fiddles were in attendance, and there were morris dances[75] on the elastic turf of the bowling green. In 1685 a subscription had just been raised among those who frequented the wells for building a church, which the Tories, who then domineered everywhere, insisted on dedicating to Saint Charles the Martyr.

But at the head of the English watering places, without a rival, was Bath. The springs of that city had been renowned from the days of the Romans. It had been, during many centuries, the seat of a bishop. The sick repaired thither from every part of the realm. The king sometimes held his court there. Nevertheless, Bath was then a maze of only four or five hundred houses, crowded within an old wall in the vicinity of the Avon. Pictures of what were considered as the finest of those houses are still extant, and greatly resemble the lowest rag shops and pothouses of Radcliffe

Highway. Even then, indeed, travelers complained of the
narrowness and meanness of the streets. That beautiful city,
which charms even eyes familiar with the masterpieces of
Bramante and Palladio,[76] and which the genius of Anstey and
5 of Smollett, of Frances Burney and of Jane Austen,[77] has
made classic ground, had not begun to exist. Milsom Street
itself was an open field lying far beyond the walls; and
hedgerows intersected the space which is now covered by
the Crescent and the Circus. As to the comforts and lux-
10 uries which were to be found in the interior of the houses of
Bath by the fashionable visitors who resorted thither in search
of health or amusement, we possess information more complete and minute than can generally be obtained on such
subjects. A writer who published an account of that city
15 about sixty years after the Revolution has accurately described the changes which had taken place within his own
recollection. He assures us that in his younger days the
gentlemen who visited the springs slept in rooms hardly as
good as the garrets which he lived to see occupied by foot-
20 men. The floors of the dining-rooms were uncarpeted, and
were colored brown with a wash made of soot and small
beer, in order to hide the dirt. Not a wainscot was painted.
Not a hearth or chimney-piece was of marble. A slab of
common freestone and fire irons which had cost from three
25 to four shillings were thought sufficient for any fireplace.
The best apartments were hung with coarse woolen stuff,
and were furnished with rush-bottomed chairs. Readers who
take an interest in the progress of civilization and of the
useful arts will be grateful to the humble topographer who
30 has recorded these facts, and will perhaps wish that historians of far higher pretensions had sometimes spared a few
pages from military evolutions and political intrigues for the
purpose of letting us know how the parlors and bedchambers
of our ancestors looked.

The position of London, relatively to the other towns of the empire, was, in the time of Charles the Second, far higher than at present. For at present the population of London is little more than six times the population of Manchester or of Liverpool. In the days of Charles the Second the population of London was more than seventeen times the population of Bristol or of Norwich. It may be doubted whether any other instance can be mentioned of a great kingdom in which the first city was more than seventeen times as large as the second. There is reason to believe that, in 1685, London had been, during about half a century, the most populous capital in Europe. The inhabitants, who are now at least nineteen hundred thousand, were then probably a little more than half a million.* London had in the world only one commercial rival, now long outstripped, the mighty and opulent Amsterdam. English writers boasted of the forest of masts and yard arms which covered the river from the bridge to the Tower, and of the incredible sums which were collected at the Custom-House in Thames Street. There is, indeed, no doubt that the trade of the metropolis then bore a far greater proportion than at present to the whole trade of the country; yet to our generation the honest vaunting of our ancestors must appear almost ludicrous. The shipping which they thought incredibly great appears not to have exceeded seventy thousand tons. This was, indeed, then more than a third of the whole tonnage of the kingdom, but is now less than a fourth of the tonnage of Newcastle, and is nearly equaled by the tonnage of the steam vessels of the Thames. The customs of London amounted, in 1685, to about three hundred and thirty thousand pounds a year. In our time the net duty paid annually, at the same place, exceeds ten millions.†

* According to King, 530,000.

† Macpherson's *History of Commerce.* Chalmers's estimate. **Cham-**

Whoever examines the maps of London which were published towards the close of the reign of Charles the Second
will see that only the nucleus of the present capital then
existed. The town did not, as now, fade by imperceptible
5 degrees into the country. No long avenues of villas, em-
bowered in lilacs and laburnums, extended from the great
center of wealth and civilization almost to the boundaries of
Middlesex and far into the heart of Kent and Surrey. In the
east, no part of the immense line of warehouses and artificial
10 lakes which now spreads from the Tower to Blackwall had
even been projected. On the west, scarcely one of those
stately piles of building which are inhabited by the noble
and wealthy was in existence; and Chelsea, which is now
peopled by more than forty thousand human beings, was a
15 quiet country village with scarce a thousand inhabitants.
On the north, cattle fed and sportsmen wandered with dogs
and guns over the site of the borough of Marylebone, and
over far the greater part of the space now covered by the
boroughs of Finsbury and of the Tower Hamlets. Islington
20 was almost a solitude; and poets loved to contrast its silence
and repose with the din and turmoil of the monster London.
On the south, the capital is now connected with its suburb
by several bridges, not inferior in magnificence and solidity
to the noblest works of the Cæsars. In 1685 a single line
25 of irregular arches, overhung by piles of mean and crazy
houses, and garnished after a fashion worthy of the naked
barbarians of Dahomy, with scores of mouldering heads,
impeded the navigation of the river.

Of the metropolis, the City, properly so called, was the
30 most important division. At the time of the Restoration it

berlayne's *State of England, 1684.* The tonnage of the steamers
belonging to the port of London was, at the end of 1847, about 60,000
tons. The customs of the port, from 1842 to 1845, very nearly averaged
£11,000,000.

had been built, for the most part, of wood and plaster ; the few bricks that were used were ill baked ; the booths where goods were exposed to sale projected far into the streets, and were overhung by the upper stories.   A few specimens of this architecture may still be seen in those districts which 5 were not reached by the great fire.   That fire had, in a few days, covered a space of little less than a square mile with the ruins of eighty-nine churches and of thirteen thousand houses.   But the city had risen again with a celerity which had excited the admiration of neighboring countries.   Unfor- 10 tunately, the old lines of the streets had been to a great extent preserved; and those lines, originally traced in an age when even princesses performed their journeys on horseback, were often too narrow to allow wheeled carriages to pass each other with ease, and were therefore ill adapted for the 15 residence of wealthy persons in an age when a coach and six was a fashionable luxury.   The style of building was, how- ever, far superior to that of the city which had perished. The ordinary material was brick, of much better quality than had formerly been used.   On the sites of the ancient parish 20 churches had arisen a multitude of new domes, towers, and spires which bore the mark of the fertile genius of Wren. In every place save one the traces of the great devastation had been completely effaced.   But the crowds of workmen, the scaffolds, and the masses of hewn stone were still to be 25 seen where the noblest of Protestant temples was slowly rising on the ruins of the old cathedral of St. Paul.

The whole character of the City has, since that time, undergone a complete change.   At present the bankers, the merchants, and the chief shopkeepers repair thither on six 30 mornings of every week for the transaction of business; but they reside in other quarters of the metropolis, or at suburban country-seats surrounded by shrubberies and flower gardens. This revolution in private habits has produced a political

revolution of no small importance. The City is no longer
regarded by the wealthiest traders with that attachment which
every man naturally feels for his home. It is no longer
associated in their minds with domestic affections and
5 endearments. The fireside, the nursery, the social table,
the quiet bed are not there. Lombard Street and Thread-
needle Street are merely places where men toil and accumulate. They go elsewhere to enjoy and to expend. On a
Sunday or in an evening after the hours of business, some
10 courts and alleys, which a few hours before had been alive
with hurrying feet and anxious faces, are as silent as a country churchyard. The chiefs of the mercantile interest are
no longer citizens. They avoid, they almost contemn, municipal honors and duties. Those honors and duties are aban-
15 doned to men who, though useful and highly respectable,
seldom belong to the princely commercial houses of which
the names are held in honor throughout the world.

In the seventeenth century the City was the merchant's
residence. Those mansions of the great old burghers which
20 still exist have been turned into counting-houses and warehouses ; but it is evident that they were originally not inferior
in magnificence to the dwellings which were then inhabited
by the nobility. They sometimes stand in retired and gloomy
courts, and are accessible only by inconvenient passages; but
25 their dimensions are ample and their aspect stately. The
entrances are decorated with richly carved pillars and can-
opies. The staircases and landing-places are not wanting in
grandeur. The floors are sometimes of wood, tessellated
after the fashion of France. The palace of Sir Robert
30 Clayton, in the Old Jewry, contained a superb banqueting
room wainscoted with cedar and adorned with battles of
gods and giants in fresco. Sir Dudley North expended four
thousand pounds, a sum which would then have been important to a duke, on the rich furniture of his reception rooms

in Basinghall Street. In such abodes, under the last Stuarts, the heads of the great firms lived splendidly and hospitably. To their dwelling-place they were bound by the strongest ties of interest and affection. There they had passed their youth, had made their friendships, had courted their wives, 5 had seen their children grow up, had laid the remains of their parents in the earth, and expected that their own remains would be laid. That intense patriotism which is peculiar to the members of societies congregated within a narrow space was, in such circumstances, strongly developed. London 10 was, to the Londoner, what Athens was to the Athenian of the age of Pericles, what Florence was to the Florentine of the fifteenth century. The citizen was proud of the grandeur of his city, punctilious about her claims to respect, ambitious of her offices, and zealous for her franchises. 15

At the close of the reign of Charles the Second the pride of the Londoners was smarting from a cruel mortification. The old charter had been taken away, and the magistracy had been remodelled. All the civic functionaries were Tories; and the Whigs, though in numbers and in wealth 20 superior to their opponents, found themselves excluded from every local dignity. Nevertheless, the external splendor of the municipal government was not diminished, nay, was rather increased by this change. For, under the adminis-tration of some Puritans who had lately borne rule, the 25 ancient fame of the City for good cheer had declined; but under the new magistrates, who belonged to a more festive party, and at whose boards guests of rank and fashion from beyond Temple Bar were often seen, the Guildhall and the halls of the great companies were enlivened by many sump- 30 tuous banquets. During these repasts, odes, composed by the poet laureate of the corporation, in praise of the king, the duke, and the mayor, were sung to music. The drinking was deep, the shouting loud. An observant Tory, who had often shared in these revels, has remarked that the practice of huzzaing after drinking healths dates from this joyous period.

The magnificence displayed by the first civic magistrate 5 was almost regal. The gilded coach, indeed, which is now annually admired by the crowd, was not yet a part of his state. On great occasions he appeared on horseback, attended by a long cavalcade inferior in magnificence only to that which, before a coronation, escorted the sovereign from 10 the Tower to Westminster. The Lord Mayor was never seen in public without his rich robe, his hood of black velvet, his gold chain, his jewel, and a great attendance of harbingers and guards. Nor did the world find anything ludicrous in the pomp which constantly surrounded him. For 15 it was not more than proportioned to the place which, as wielding the strength and representing the dignity of the city of London, he was entitled to occupy in the state. That city, being then not only without equal in the country, but without second, had, during five and forty years, exercised 20 almost as great an influence on the politics of England as Paris has, in our own time, exercised on the politics of France. In intelligence London was greatly in advance of every other part of the kingdom. A government, supported and trusted by London, could in a day obtain such pecuniary 25 means as it would have taken months to collect from the rest of the island. Nor were the military resources of the capital to be despised. The power which the lord lieutenants exercised in other parts of the kingdom was in London intrusted to a commission of eminent citizens. Under the orders of 30 this commission were twelve regiments of foot and two regiments of horse. An army of drapers' apprentices and journeymen tailors, with common councilmen for captains and aldermen for colonels, might not indeed have been able to stand its ground against regular troops; but there were then very few regular troops in the kingdom. A town, therefore, which could send forth, at an hour's notice, twenty thousand men, abounding in natural courage, provided with tolerable weapons, and not altogether untinctured with martial discipline, could not but be a valuable ally and a formidable 5 enemy. It was not forgotten that Hampden and Pym [78] had been protected from lawless tyranny by the London trainbands; that, in the great crisis of the Civil War, the London trainbands had marched to raise the siege of Gloucester; or that, in the movement against the military tyrants which fol- 10 lowed the downfall of Richard Cromwell,[79] the London trainbands had borne a signal part. In truth, it is no exaggeration to say that, but for the hostility of the City, Charles the First would never have been vanquished, and that, without the help of the City, Charles the Second could scarcely have 15 been restored.

These considerations may serve to explain why, in spite of that attraction which had, during a long course of years, gradually drawn the aristocracy westward, a few men of high rank had continued, till a very recent period, to dwell in the 20 vicinity of the Exchange and of the Guildhall. Shaftesbury [80] and Buckingham, while engaged in bitter and unscrupulous opposition to the government, had thought that they could nowhere carry on their intrigues so conveniently or so securely as under the protection of the city magistrates 25 and the city militia. Shaftesbury had therefore lived in Aldersgate Street, at a house which may still easily be known by pilasters and wreaths, the graceful work of Inigo.[81] Buckingham had ordered his mansion near Charing Cross, once the abode of the archbishops of York, to 30 be pulled down ; and, while streets and alleys which are still named after him were rising on that site, chose to reside in Dowgate.

These, however, were rare exceptions. Almost all the

noble families of England had long migrated beyond the
walls.   The district where most of their town houses stood
lies between the city and the regions which are now considered as fashionable.   A few great men still retained their
5 hereditary hotels between the Strand and the river.   The
stately dwellings on the south and west of Lincoln's Inn
Fields, the Piazza of Covent Garden, Southampton Square,
which is now called Bloomsbury Square, and King's Square
in Soho Fields, which is now called Soho Square, were
10 among the favorite spots.   Foreign princes were carried to
see Bloomsbury Square as one of the wonders of England.
Soho Square, which had just been built, was to our ancestors a subject of pride with which their posterity will hardly
sympathize.   Monmouth Square had been the name while
15 the fortunes of the Duke of Monmouth flourished, and on
the southern side towered his mansion.   The front, though
ungraceful, was lofty and richly adorned.   The walls of the
principal apartments were finely sculptured with fruit, foliage,
and armorial bearings, and were hung with embroidered
20 satin.   Every trace of this magnificence has long disappeared, and no aristocratical mansion is to be found in that
once aristocratical quarter.   A little way north from Hol-
born, and on the verge of the pastures and cornfields, rose
two celebrated palaces, each with an ample garden.   One of
25 them, then called Southampton House and subsequently Bed-
ford House, was removed about fifty years ago to make room
for a new city, which now covers, with its squares, streets,
and churches, a vast area, renowned in the seventeenth
century for peaches and snipes.   The other, Montague
30 House, celebrated for its frescoes and furniture, was, a few
months after the death of Charles the Second, burned to the
ground, and was speedily succeeded by a more magnificent
Montague House, which, having been long the repository .
of such various and precious treasures of art, science, and

learning as were scarce ever before assembled under a single roof, has just given place to an edifice more magnificent still.

Nearer to the court, on a space called Saint James's Fields, had just been built Saint James's Square and Jermyn 5 Street. Saint James's Church had recently been opened for the accommodation of the inhabitants of this new quarter. Golden Square, which was in the next generation inhabited by lords and ministers of state, had not yet been begun. Indeed the only dwellings to be seen on the north 10 of Piccadilly were three or four isolated and almost rural mansions, of which the most celebrated was the costly pile erected by Clarendon, and nicknamed Dunkirk House. It had been purchased after its founder's downfall by the Duke of Albemarle. The Clarendon Hotel and Albemarle Street 15 still preserve the memory of the site.

He who then rambled to what is now the gayest and most crowded part of Regent Street found himself in a solitude, and was sometimes so fortunate as to have a shot at a woodcock.* On the north the Oxford Road ran between 20 hedges. Three or four hundred yards to the south were the garden walls of a few great houses, which were considered as quite out of town. On the west was a meadow renowned for a spring from which, long afterwards, Conduit Street was named. On the east was a field not to be passed 25 without a shudder by any Londoner of that age. There, as in a place far from the haunts of men, had been dug, twenty years before, when the great plague was raging, a pit into which the dead carts had nightly shot corpses by scores. It was popularly believed that the earth was deeply tainted 30 with infection, and could not be disturbed without imminent risk to human life. No foundations were laid there till two

* Old General Oglethorpe, who lived to 1785, used to boast that he had shot here in Anne's reign.

generations had passed without any return of the pestilence, and till the ghastly spot had long been surrounded by buildings.*

We should greatly err if we were to suppose that any of 5 the streets and squares then bore the same aspect as at present. The great majority of the houses, indeed, have, since that time, been wholly or in great part rebuilt. If the most fashionable parts of the capital could be placed before us, such as they then were, we should be disgusted 10 by their squalid appearance and poisoned by their noisome atmosphere. In Covent Garden a filthy and noisy market was held close to the dwellings of the great. Fruit women screamed, carters fought, cabbage stalks and rotten apples accumulated in heaps at the thresholds of the Countess of 15 Berkshire and of the Bishop of Durham.

The center of Lincoln's Inn Fields was an open space where the rabble congregated every evening, within a few yards of Cardigan House and Winchester House, to hear mountebanks harangue, to see bears dance, and to set dogs at 20 oxen. Rubbish was shot in every part of the area. Horses were exercised there. The beggars were as noisy and importunate as in the worst governed cities of the Continent. A Lincoln's Inn mumper was a proverb. The whole fraternity knew the arms and liveries of every charitably disposed 25 grandee in the neighborhood, and, as soon as his lordship's coach and six appeared, came hopping and crawling in crowds to persecute him. These disorders lasted, in spite of many accidents and of some legal proceedings, till, in the reign of George the Second, Sir Joseph Jekyll, Master of the 30 Rolls, was knocked down and nearly killed in the middle of the square. Then at length palisades were set up and a pleasant garden laid out.

* The pest field will be seen in maps of London as late as the end of George the First's reign.

Saint James's Square was a receptacle for all the offal and cinders, for all the dead cats and dead dogs of Westminster. At one time a cudgel player kept the ring there. At another time an impudent squatter settled himself there, and built a shed for rubbish under the windows of the gilded saloons in which the first magnates of the realm, Norfolks, Ormonds, Kents, and Pembrokes, gave banquets and balls. It was not till these nuisances had lasted through a whole generation and till much had been written about them that the inhabitants applied to parliament for permission to put up rails and to plant trees.

When such was the state of the quarter inhabited by the most luxurious portion of society, we may easily believe that the great body of the population suffered what would now be considered as insupportable grievances. The pavement was detestable; all foreigners cried shame upon it. The drainage was so bad that in rainy weather the gutters soon became torrents. Several facetious poets have commemorated the fury with which these black rivulets roared down Snow Hill and Ludgate Hill, bearing to Fleet Ditch a vast tribute of animal and vegetable filth from the stalls of butchers and greengrocers. This flood was profusely thrown to right and left by coaches and carts. To keep as far from the carriage road as possible was therefore the wish of every pedestrian. The mild and timid gave the wall. The bold and athletic took it. If two roisters met, they cocked their hats in each other's faces and pushed each other about till the weaker was shoved towards the kennel. If he was a mere bully he sneaked off, muttering that he should find a time. If he was pugnacious, the encounter probably ended in a duel behind Montague House.

The houses were not numbered. There would indeed have been little advantage in numbering them; for of the coachmen, chairmen, porters, and errand boys of London, a very small portion could read. It was necessary to use marks which the most ignorant could understand. The shops were therefore distinguished by painted signs, which gave a gay and grotesque aspect to the streets. The walk 5 from Charing Cross to Whitechapel lay through an endless succession of Saracen's Heads, Royal Oaks, Blue Bears, and Golden Lambs, which disappeared when they were no longer required for the direction of the common people.

When the evening closed in, the difficulty and danger of 10 walking about London became serious indeed. The garret windows were opened, and pails were emptied, with little regard to those who were passing below. Falls, bruises, and broken bones were of constant occurrence. For, till the last year of the reign of Charles the Second, most of the streets 15 were left in profound darkness. Thieves and robbers plied their trade with impunity ; yet they were hardly so terrible to peaceable citizens as another class of ruffians. It was a favorite amusement of dissolute young gentlemen to swagger by night about the town, breaking windows, upsetting 20 sedans, beating quiet men, and offering rude caresses to pretty women. Several dynasties of these tyrants had, since the Restoration, domineered over the streets. The Muns and Tityre Tus had given place to the Hectors, and the Hectors had been recently succeeded by the Scourers. At 25 a later period arose the Nicker, the Hawcubite, and the yet more dreaded name of Mohawk.* The machinery for keep-

---

* It may be suspected that some of the Tityre Tus, like good Cavaliers, broke Milton's windows shortly after the Restoration. I am confident that he was thinking of those pests of London when he dictated
30 the noble lines, —

"And in luxurious cities, when the noise
Of riot ascends above their loftiest towers,
And injury and outrage, and when night
Darkens the streets, then wander forth the sons
35   Of Belial, flown with insolence and wine."

ing the peace was utterly contemptible.   There was an act
of Common Council which provided that more than a thousand watchmen should be constantly on the alert in the city,
from sunset to sunrise, and that every inhabitant should take
his turn of duty.   But the act was negligently executed.   5
Few of those who were summoned left their homes ; and
those few generally found it more agreeable to tipple in alehouses than to pace the streets.

It ought to be noticed that, in the last year of the reign of
Charles the Second, began a great change in the police 10
of London, — a change which has perhaps added as much to
the happiness of the great body of the people as revolutions
of much greater fame.   An ingenious projector, named
Edward Heming, obtained letters patent conveying to him,
for a term of years, the exclusive right of lighting up London. 15
He undertook, for a moderate consideration, to place a light
before every tenth door, on moonless nights, from Michaelmas to Lady Day, and from six to twelve of the clock.
Those who now see the capital all the year round, from dusk
to dawn, blazing with a splendor compared with which the 20
illuminations for La Hogue and Blenheim would have looked
pale, may perhaps smile to think of Heming's lanterns, which
glimmered feebly before one house in ten during a small
part of one night in three.   But such was not the feeling
of his contemporaries.   His scheme was enthusiastically 25
applauded and furiously attacked.   The friends of improvement extolled him as the greatest of all the benefactors of
his city.   What, they asked, were the boasted inventions
of Archimedes when compared with the achievement of the
man who had turned the nocturnal shades into noonday ? 30
In spite of these eloquent eulogies, the cause of darkness
was not left undefended.   There were fools in that age who
opposed the introduction of what was called the new light
as strenuously as fools in our age have opposed the intro-

duction of vaccination and railroads, as strenuously as the
fools of an age anterior to the dawn of history doubtless
opposed the introduction of the plough and of alphabetical
writing. Many years after the date of Heming's patent,
5 there were extensive districts in which no lamp was seen.

We may easily imagine what, in such times, must have
been the state of the quarters peopled by the outcasts of
society. Among those quarters one had attained a scandalous preëminence. On the confines of the city and the
10 Temple had been founded, in the thirteenth century, a
House of Carmelite Friars, distinguished by their white
hoods. The precinct of this house had, before the Reformation, been a sanctuary for criminals, and still retained the
privilege of protecting debtors from arrest. Insolvents con-
15 sequently were to be found in every dwelling, from cellar to
garret. Of these a large proportion were knaves and libertines, and were followed to their asylum by women more
abandoned than themselves. The civil power was unable to
keep order in a district swarming with such inhabitants;
20 and thus Whitefriars became the favorite resort of all who
wished to be emancipated from the restraints of the law.
Though the immunities legally belonging to the place extended only to cases of debt, cheats, false witnesses, forgers,
and highwaymen found refuge there. For amidst a rabble
25 so desperate no peace officer's life was in safety. At the
cry of " Rescue," bullies with swords and cudgels and ter-
magant hags with spits and broomsticks poured forth by
hundreds; and the intruder was fortunate if he escaped
back into Fleet Street, hustled, stripped, and pumped upon.
30 Even the warrant of the Chief Justice of England could not
be executed without the help of a company of musketeers.
Such relics of the barbarism of the darkest ages were to be
found within a short walk of the chambers where Somers [8]
was studying history and law, of the chapel where Tillot

son[88] was preaching, of the coffee-house where Dryden[84] was
passing judgment on poems and plays, and of the hall where
the Royal Society was examining the astronomical system
of Isaac Newton.[85]

Each of the two cities which made up the capital of Eng-   5
land had its own center of attraction. In the metropolis
of commerce the point of convergence was the Exchange;
in the metropolis of fashion the Palace. But the Palace did
not retain its influence so long as the Exchange. The
revolution completely altered the relations between the court 10
and the higher classes of society. It was by degrees discovered that the king, in his individual capacity, had very
little to give; that coronets and garters, bishoprics, and em-
bassies, lordships of the treasury, and tellerships of the
Exchequer, nay, even charges in the royal stud and bed-   15
chamber, were really bestowed, not by the king, but by his
advisers. Every ambitious and covetous man perceived that
he would consult his own interest far better by acquiring
the dominion of a Cornish borough, and by rendering good
service to the ministry during a critical session, than by be- 20
coming the companion or even the minion of his prince. It
was therefore in the antechambers, not of George the First
and of George the Second, but of Walpole and of Pelham,
that the daily crowd of courtiers was to be found.[86] It is
also to be remarked that the same revolution which made 25
it impossible that our kings should use the patronage of the
state, merely for the purpose of gratifying their personal
predilections, gave us several kings unfitted by their education and habits to be gracious and affable hosts.   They had
been born and bred on the Continent. They never felt 30
themselves at home in our island. If they spoke our language they spoke it inelegantly and with effort. Our national
character they never fully understood. Our national manners they hardly attempted to acquire. The most important

part of their duty they performed better than any ruler who
had preceded them, for they governed strictly according to
law ; but they could not be the first gentlemen of the realm,
the heads of polite society.   If ever they unbent it was in a
5 very small circle, where hardly an English face was to be
seen ; and they were never so happy as when they could
escape for a summer to their native land.   They had indeed
their days of reception for our nobility and gentry ; but the
reception was mere matter of form, and became at last as
10 solemn a ceremony as a funeral.

Not such was the court of Charles the Second.   Whitehall, when he dwelt there, was the focus of political intrigue
and of fashionable gayety.   Half the jobbing and half the
flirting of the metropolis went on under his roof.   Whoever
15 could make himself agreeable to the prince or could secure
the good offices of the mistress might hope to rise in the
world without rendering any service to the government, without being even known by sight to any minister of state.
This courtier got a frigate, and that a company; a third, the
20 pardon of a rich offender; a fourth, a lease of crown land
on easy terms.   If the king notified his pleasure that a brief-
less lawyer should be made a judge or that a libertine baronet should be made a peer, the gravest councillors, after
a little murmuring, submitted.   Interest, therefore, drew a
25 constant press of suitors to the gates of the palace, and
those gates always stood wide.   The king kept open house
every day, and all day long, for the good society of London,
the extreme Whigs only excepted.   Hardly any gentleman
had any difficulty in making his way to the royal presence.
30 The levee was exactly what the word imports.   Some men
of quality came every morning to stand round their master,
to chat with him while his wig was combed and his cravat
tied, and to accompany him in his early walk through the
park.   All persons who had been properly introduced might,

without any special invitation, go to see him dine, sup, dance, and play at hazard, and might have the pleasure of hearing him tell stories, which, indeed, he told remarkably well, about his flight from Worcester,[87] and about the misery which he had endured when he was a state prisoner in the hands of the canting, meddling preachers of Scotland. Bystanders whom his majesty recognized often came in for a courteous word. This proved a far more successful kingcraft than any that his father or grandfather had practised. It was not easy for the most austere republican of the school of Marvel[88] to resist the fascination of so much good humor and affability; and many a veteran Cavalier, in whose heart the remembrance of unrequited sacrifices and services had been festering during a quarter of a century, was compensated in one moment for wounds and sequestrations by his sovereign's kind nod, and "God bless you, my old friend!"

Whitehall naturally became the chief staple of news. Whenever there was a rumor that anything important had happened or was about to happen, people hastened thither to obtain intelligence from the fountain head. The galleries presented the appearance of a modern clubroom at an anxious time. They were full of people inquiring whether the Dutch mail was in, what tidings the express from France had brought, whether John Sobiesky had beaten the Turks, whether the Doge of Genoa was really at Paris. These were matters about which it was safe to talk aloud. But there were subjects concerning which information was asked and given in whispers. Had Halifax got the better of Rochester?[89] Was there to be a parliament? Was the Duke of York really going to Scotland? Had Monmouth[90] really been sent for to the Hague? Men tried to read the countenance of every minister as he went through the throng to and from the royal closet. All sorts of auguries were drawn from the tone in which his majesty spoke to the Lord Presi-

dent, or from the laugh with which his majesty honored a
jest of the Lord Privy Seal ; and, in a few hours, the hopes
and fears inspired by such slight indications had spread to
all the coffee-houses from St. James's to the Tower.

5   The coffee-house must not be dismissed with a cursory
mention.   It might indeed, at that time, have been not
improperly called a most important political institution.   No
parliament had sate for years.   The municipal council of the
city had ceased to speak the sense of the citizens.   Public
10 meetings, harangues, resolutions, and the rest of the modern
machinery of agitation had not yet come into fashion.
Nothing resembling the modern newspaper existed.   In such
circumstances, the coffee-houses were the chief organs
through which the public opinion of the metropolis vented
15 itself.

The first of these establishments had been set up, in the
time of the Commonwealth, by a Turkey merchant, who had
acquired among the Mahometans a taste for their favorite
beverage.   The convenience of being able to make appoint-
20 ments in any part of the town, and of being able to pass
evenings socially at a very small charge, was so great that
the fashion spread fast.   Every man of the upper or middle
class went daily to his coffee-house to learn the news and to
discuss it.   Every coffee-house had one or more orators to
25 whose eloquence the crowd listened with admiration, and
who soon became, what the journalists of our own time have
been called, a fourth estate of the realm.   The court had
long seen with uneasiness the growth of this new power in
the state.   An attempt had been made, during Danby's
30 administration, to close the coffee-houses.   But men of all
parties missed their usual places of resort so much that there
was a universal outcry.   The government did not venture, in
opposition to a feeling so strong and general, to enforce a
regulation of which the legality might well be questioned.

Since that time ten years had elapsed, and, during those years, the number and influence of the coffee-houses had been constantly increasing. Foreigners remarked that the coffee-house was that which especially distinguished London from all other cities; that the coffee-house was the Londoner's home, and that those who wished to find a gentleman commonly asked, not whether he lived in Fleet Street or Chancery Lane, but whether he frequented the Grecian or the Rainbow. Nobody was excluded from these places who laid down his penny at the bar. Yet every rank and profession and every shade of religious and political opinion had its own headquarters. There were houses near St. James's Park where fops congregated, their heads and shoulders covered with black or flaxen wigs, not less ample than those which are now worn by the chancellor and by the speaker of the House of Commons. The wig came from Paris, and so did the rest of the fine gentleman's ornaments, his embroidered coat, his fringed gloves, and the tassel which upheld his pantaloons. The conversation was in that dialect which, long after it had ceased to be spoken in fashionable circles, continued, in the mouth of Lord Foppington,[91] to excite the mirth of theatres. The atmosphere was like that of a perfumer's shop. Tobacco in any other form than that of richly scented snuff was held in abomination. If any clown, ignorant of the usages of the house, called for a pipe, the sneers of the whole assembly and the short answers of the waiters soon convinced him that he had better go somewhere else. Nor, indeed, would he have had far to go. For, in general, the coffee-rooms reeked with tobacco like a guard room; and strangers sometimes expressed their surprise that so many people should leave their own firesides to sit in the midst of eternal fog and stench. Nowhere was the smoking more constant than at Will's. That celebrated house, situated between Covent Garden and Bow Street, was sacred to

polite letters. There the talk was about poetical justice and
the unities of place and time. There was a faction for
Perrault [92] and the moderns, a faction for Boileau [93] and the
ancients. One group debated whether *Paradise Lost* ought
5 not to have been in rhyme. To another an envious poetaster
demonstrated that *Venice Preserved* [94] ought to have been
hooted from the stage. Under no roof was a greater variety
of figures to be seen, — earls in stars and garters, clergymen
in cassocks and bands, pert templars, sheepish lads from the
10 universities, translators and index-makers in ragged coats of
frieze. The great press was to get near the chair where
John Dryden sate. In winter, that chair was always in the
warmest nook by the fire; in summer, it stood in the balcony.
To bow to him, and to hear his opinion of Racine's last
15 tragedy or of Bossu's [95] treatise on epic poetry, was thought
a privilege. A pinch from his snuff-box was an honor sufficient to turn the head of a young enthusiast. There were
coffee-houses where the first medical men might be consulted.
Doctor John Radcliffe, who, in the year 1685, rose to the
20 largest practice in London, came daily, at the hour when the
Exchange was full, from his house in Bow Street, then a
fashionable part of the capital, to Garraway's, and was to be
found surrounded by surgeons and apothecaries at a particular table. There were Puritan coffee-houses where no oath
25 was heard, and where lank-haired men discussed election
and reprobation through their noses ; Jew coffee-houses
where dark-eyed money-changers from Venice and Amsterdam greeted each other; and Popish coffee-houses where,
as good Protestants believed, Jesuits planned, over their
30 cups, another great fire, and cast silver bullets to shoot the
king.

These gregarious habits had no small share in forming
the character of the Londoner of that age. He was, indeed,
a different being from the rustic Englishman. There was

not then the intercourse which now exists between the two
classes.   Only very great men were in the habit of dividing
the year between town and country.   Few esquires came to
the capital thrice in their lives.   Nor was it yet the practice
of all citizens in easy circumstances to breathe the fresh air   5
of the fields and woods during some weeks of every summer.
A cockney, in a rural village, was stared at as much as if he
had intruded into a Kraal of Hottentots.   On the other
hand, when the lord of a Lincolnshire or Shropshire manor
appeared in Fleet Street, he was as easily distinguished 10
from the resident population as a Turk or a Lascar.   His
dress, his gait, his accent, the manner in which he stared at
the shops, stumbled into the gutters, ran against the porters,
and stood under the waterspouts marked him out as an excellent subject for the operations of swindlers and banterers. 15
Bullies jostled him into the kennel.   Hackney coachmen
splashed him from head to foot.   Thieves explored with
perfect security the huge pockets of his horseman's coat,
while he stood entranced by the splendor of the Lord
Mayor's show.   Money-droppers, sore from the cart's tail, 20
introduced themselves to him, and appeared to him the
most honest, friendly gentlemen that he had ever seen.
Painted women, the refuse of Lewkner Lane and Whetstone
Park, passed themselves on him for countesses and maids of
honor.   If he asked his way to St. James's, his informants 25
sent him to Mile End.   If he went into a shop, he was
instantly discerned to be a fit purchaser of everything that
nobody else would buy, of second-hand embroidery, copper
rings, and watches that would not go.   If he rambled into
any fashionable coffee-house, he became a mark for the inso- 30
lent derision of fops and the grave waggery of templars.
Enraged and mortified, he soon returned to his mansion,
and there, in the homage of his tenants and the conversation of his boon companions, found consolation for the vexa-

tions and humiliations which he had undergone.   There he once more felt himself a great man ; and he saw nothing above him except when at the assizes he took his seat on the bench near the judge or when at the muster of the
5 militia he saluted the lord lieutenant.

The chief cause which made the fusion of the different elements of society so imperfect was the extreme difficulty which our ancestors found in passing from place to place. Of all inventions, the alphabet and the printing-press alone
10 excepted, those inventions which abridge distance have done most for the civilization of our species.   Every improvement of the means of locomotion benefits mankind morally and intellectually as well as materially, and not only facilitates the interchange of the various productions of nature and
15 art, but tends to remove national and provincial antipathies, and to bind together all the branches of the great human family.   In the seventeenth century the inhabitants of London were, for almost every practical purpose, further from Reading than they now are from Edinburgh, and further
20 from Edinburgh than they now are from Vienna.

The subjects of Charles the Second were not, it is true, quite unacquainted with that principle which has, in our own time, produced an unprecedented revolution in human affairs, which has enabled navies to advance in the face of
25 wind and tide, and battalions, attended by all their baggage and artillery, to traverse kingdoms at a pace equal to that of the fleetest race horse.   The Marquess of Worcester had recently observed the expansive power of moisture rarefied by heat.   After many experiments he had succeeded in con-
30 structing a rude steam engine, which he called a fire water work, and which he pronounced to be an admirable and most forcible instrument of propulsion.   But the marquess was suspected to be a madman and known to be a Papist. His inventions, therefore, found no favorable reception.

His fire water work might, perhaps, furnish matter for conversation at a meeting of the Royal Society, but was not
applied to any practical purpose.   There were no railways,
except a few made of timber, from the mouths of the North-
umbrian coal pits to the banks of the Tyne.   There was 5
very little internal communication by water.   A few attempts
had been made to deepen and embank the natural streams,
but with slender success.   Hardly a single navigable canal
had been even projected.   The English of that day were in
the habit of talking with mingled admiration and despair of 10
the immense trench by which Louis the Fourteenth had
made a junction between the Atlantic and the Mediterranean.   They little thought that their country would, in the
course of a few generations, be intersected, at the cost of
private adventures, by artificial rivers making up more than 15
four times the length of the Thames, the Severn, and the
Trent together.

It was by the highways that both travelers and goods generally passed from place to place.   And those highways appear to have been far worse than might have been expected 20
from the degree of wealth and civilization which the nation
had even then attained.   On the best lines of communication the ruts were deep, the descents precipitous, and the
way often such as it was hardly possible to distinguish, in
the dusk, from the unenclosed heath and fen which lay on 25
both sides.   Ralph Thoresby, the antiquary, was in danger
of losing his way on the great North Road, between Barnby
Moor and Tuxford, and actually lost it between Doncaster
and York.   Pepys and his wife, traveling in their own coach,
lost their way between Newbury and Reading.   In the 30
course of the same tour they lost their way near Salisbury,
and were in danger of having to pass the night on the plain.
It was only in fine weather that the whole breadth of the
road was available for wheeled vehicles.   Often the mud

lay deep on the right and the left, and only a narrow track
of firm ground rose above the quagmire. At such times
obstructions and quarrels were frequent, and the path was
sometimes blocked up during a long time by carriers, neither
5 of whom would break the way. It happened almost every
day that coaches stuck fast until a team of cattle could be
procured from some neighboring farm to tug them out of
the slough. But in bad seasons the traveler had to encounter inconveniences still more serious. Thoresby, who
10 was in the habit of traveling between Leeds and the capital,
has recorded, in his Diary, such a series of perils and disas-
ters as might suffice for a journey to the Frozen Ocean or
to the Desert of Sahara. On one occasion he learned that
the floods were out between Ware and London, that passen-
15 gers had to swim for their lives, and that a higgler had
perished in the attempt to cross. In consequence of these
tidings he turned out of the high road and was conducted
across some meadows, where it was necessary for him to
ride to the saddle skirts in water. In the course of another
20 journey he narrowly escaped being swept away by an inun-
dation of the Trent. He was afterwards detained at Stam-
ford four days on account of the state of the roads, and
then ventured to proceed only because fourteen members of
the House of Commons, who were going up in a body to
25 parliament with guides and numerous attendants, took him
into their company. On the roads of Derbyshire travelers
were in constant fear for their necks, and were frequently
compelled to alight and lead their beasts. The great route
through Wales to Holyhead was in such a state that, in
30 1685, a viceroy, on his road to Ireland, was five hours in
traveling fourteen miles, from Saint Asaph to Conway.
Between Conway and Beaumaris he was forced to walk a
great part of the way, and his lady was carried in a litter.
His coach was, with great difficulty and by the help of

many hands, brought after him entire. In general, carriages were taken to pieces at Conway and borne, on the
shoulders of stout Welsh peasants, to the Menai Straits.
In some parts of Kent and Sussex none but the strongest
horses could, in winter, get through the bog, in which, at 5
every step, they sank deep. The markets were often inac-
cessible during several months. It is said that the fruits of
the earth were sometimes suffered to rot in one place, while
in another place, distant only a few miles, the supply fell
far short of the demand. The wheeled carriages were, in 10
this district, generally pulled by oxen. When Prince George
of Denmark visited the stately mansion of Petworth in wet
weather, he was six hours in going nine miles ; and it was
necessary that a body of sturdy hinds should be on each
side of his coach in order to prop it. Of the carriages 15
which conveyed his retinue several were upset and injured.
A letter from one of his gentlemen in waiting has been preserved, in which the unfortunate courtier complains that,
during fourteen hours, he never once alighted, except when
his coach was overturned or stuck fast in the mud.   20

One chief cause of the badness of the roads seems to have
been the defective state of the law. Every parish was bound
to repair the highways which passed through it. The peasantry were forced to give their gratuitous labor six days in
the year. If this was not sufficient hired labor was employed, 25
and the expense was met by a parochial rate. That a route
connecting two great towns, which have a large and thriving
trade with each other, should be maintained at the cost of
the rural population scattered between them is obviously
unjust; and this injustice was peculiarly glaring in the case 30
of the great North Road, which traversed very poor and
thinly inhabited districts, and joined very rich and populous
districts. Indeed it was not in the power of the parishes of
Huntingdonshire to mend a highway worn by the constant

passing and repassing of traffic between the West Riding of
Yorkshire and London.   Soon after the Restoration this
grievance attracted the notice of parliament; and an act, the
first of our many turnpike acts, was passed, imposing a small
5 toll on travelers and goods, for the purpose of keeping some
parts of this important line of communication in good repair.
This innovation, however, excited many murmurs, and the
other great avenues to the capital were long left under the
old system.   A change was at length effected, but not with-
10 out great difficulty. For unjust and absurd taxation to which
men are accustomed is often borne far more willingly than
the most reasonable impost which is new.   It was not till
many toll bars had been violently pulled down, till the troops
had in many districts been forced to act against the people,
15 and till much blood had been shed that a good system was
introduced.   By slow degrees reason triumphed over prejudice; and our island is now crossed in every direction by
near thirty thousand miles of turnpike road.
    On the best highways heavy articles were, in the time of
20 Charles the Second, generally conveyed from place to place
by stage wagons.   In the straw of these vehicles nestled a
crowd of passengers, who could not afford to travel by coach
or on horseback, and who were prevented by infirmity, or by
the weight of their luggage from going on foot.   The expense
25 of transmitting heavy goods in this way was enormous.
From London to Birmingham the charge was seven pounds
a ton; from London to Exeter twelve pounds a ton.   This
was about fifteen pence a ton for every mile, more by a third
than was afterwards charged on turnpike roads, and fifteen
30 times what is now demanded by railway companies.   The
cost of conveyance amounted to a prohibitory tax on many
useful articles.   Coal in particular was never seen except in the districts where it was produced or in the
districts to which it could be carried by sea, and was

indeed always known in the south of England by the name of sea coal.

On byroads, and generally throughout the country north of York and west of Exeter, goods were carried by long trains of pack-horses. These strong and patient beasts, the 5 breed of which is now extinct, were attended by a class of men who seem to have borne much resemblance to the Spanish muleteers. A traveler of humble condition often found it convenient to perform a journey mounted on a pack-saddle between two baskets, under the care of these hardy 10 guides. The expense of this mode of conveyance was small. But the caravan moved at a foot's pace, and in winter the cold was often insupportable.

The rich commonly traveled in their own carriages, with at least four horses. Cotton, the facetious poet, attempted to 15 go from London to the Peak with a single pair, but found at St. Alban's that the journey would be insupportably tedious, and altered his plan. A coach and six is in our time never seen, except as part of some pageant. The frequent mention, therefore, of such equipages in old books is likely to mislead 20 us. We attribute to magnificence what was really the effect of a very disagreeable necessity. People, in the time of Charles the Second, traveled with six horses, because with a smaller number there was great danger of sticking fast in the mire. Nor were even six horses always sufficient. Vanbrugh, 25 in the succeeding generation, described with great humor the way in which a country gentleman, newly chosen a member of parliament, went up to London. On that occasion all the exertions of six beasts, two of which had been taken from the plough, could not save the family coach from being 30 imbedded in a quagmire.

Public carriages had recently been much improved. During the years which immediately followed the Restoration, a diligence ran between London and Oxford in two days. The

passengers slept at Beaconsfield. At length, in the spring of
1669, a great and daring innovation was attempted. It was
announced that a vehicle, described as the Flying Coach,
would perform the whole journey between sunrise and sun-
5 set. This spirited undertaking was solemnly considered and
sanctioned by the Heads of the University, and appears to
have excited the same sort of interest which is excited in our
own time by the opening of a new railway. The Vice-Chan-
cellor, by a notice which was affixed in all public places,
10 prescribed the hour and place of departure. The success of
the experiment was complete. At six in the morning the
carriage began to move from before the ancient front of All
Soul's College, and at seven in the evening the adventurous
gentlemen who had run the first risk were safely deposited
15 at their inn in London. The emulation of the sister university was moved, and soon a diligence was set up which in
one day carried passengers from Cambridge to the capital.
At the close of the reign of Charles the Second, flying carriages ran thrice a week from London to all the chief towns.
20 But no stage coach, indeed no stage wagon, appears to have
proceeded farther north than York or farther west than
Exeter. The ordinary day's journey of a flying coach was
about fifty miles in the summer; but in winter, when the
ways were bad and the nights long, little more than thirty.
25 The Chester coach, the York coach, and the Exeter coach
generally reached London in four days during the fine
season, but at Christmas not till the sixth day. The passengers, six in number, were all seated in the carriage. For
accidents were so frequent that it would have been most
30 perilous to mount the roof. The ordinary fare was about
twopence halfpenny a mile in summer, and somewhat more
in winter.

This mode of traveling, which by Englishmen of the present day would be regarded as insufferably slow, seemed to

our ancestors wonderfully and indeed alarmingly rapid. In a work published a few months before the death of Charles the Second, the flying coaches are extolled as far superior to any similar vehicles ever known in the world. Their velocity is the subject of special commendation, and is triumphantly 5 contrasted with the sluggish pace of the continental posts. But with boasts like these was mingled the sound of complaint and invective. The interests of large classes had been unfavorably affected by the establishment of the new diligences; and, as usual, many persons were, from mere stupidity 10 and obstinacy, disposed to clamor against the innovation, simply because it was an innovation. It was vehemently argued that this mode of conveyance would be fatal to the breed of horses and to the noble art of horsemanship; that the Thames, which had long been an important nursery of 15 seamen, would cease to be the chief thoroughfare from London up to Windsor and down to Gravesend; that saddlers and spurriers would be ruined by hundreds; that numerous inns, at which mounted travelers had been in the habit of stopping, would be deserted, and would no longer pay any 20 rent; that the new carriages were too hot in summer and too cold in winter; that the passengers were greviously annoyed by invalids and crying children; that the coach sometimes reached the inn so late that it was impossible to get supper, and sometimes started so early that it was impossible to get 25 breakfast. On these grounds it was gravely recommended that no public carriage should be permitted to have more than four horses, to start oftener than once a week, or to go more than thirty miles a day. It was hoped that, if this regulation were adopted, all except the sick and the lame 30 would return to the old modes of traveling. Petitions embodying such opinions as these were presented to the king in council from several companies of the city of London, from several provincial towns, and from the justices of

several counties. We smile at these things. It is not
impossible that our descendants, when they read the history
of the opposition offered by cupidity and prejudice to the
improvements of the nineteenth century, may smile in their
5 turn.

In spite of the attractions of the flying coaches, it was
still usual for men who enjoyed health and vigor, and who
were not encumbered by much baggage, to perform long
journeys on horseback. If the traveler wished to move
10 expeditiously he rode post. Fresh saddle horses and guides
were to be procured at convenient distances along all the
great lines of road. The charge was threepence a mile for
each horse and fourpence a stage for the guide. In this
manner, when the ways were good, it was possible to travel,
15 for a considerable time, as rapidly as by any conveyance
known in England, till vehicles were propelled by steam.
There were as yet no post chaises; nor could those who
rode in their own coaches ordinarily procure a change of
horses. The king, however, and the great officers of state
20 were able to command relays. Thus Charles commonly
went in one day from Whitehall to Newmarket, a distance of
about fifty-five miles through a level country; and this was
thought by his subjects a proof of great activity. Evelyn
performed the same journey in company with Lord Treasurer
25 Clifford. The coach was drawn by six horses, which were
changed at Bishop Stortford and again at Chesterford. The
travelers reached Newmarket by night. Such a mode of
conveyance seems to have been considered as a rare luxury
confined to princes and ministers.

30 Whatever might be the way in which a journey was performed, the travelers, unless they were numerous and well
armed, ran considerable risk of being stopped and plundered.
The mounted highwayman, a marauder known to our generation only from books, was to be found on every main road.

The waste tracts which lie on the great routes near London were especially haunted by plunderers of this class. Hounslow Heath, on the great Western Road, and Finchley Common, on the great Northern Road, were perhaps the most celebrated of these spots. The Cambridge scholars trembled 5 when they approached Epping Forest, even in broad daylight. Seamen who had just been paid off at Chatham were often compelled to deliver their purses on Gadshill, celebrated near a hundred years earlier by the greatest of poets as the scene of the depredations of Poins and Falstaff.[96] 10 The public authorities seem to have been often at a loss how to deal with these enterprising plunderers. At one time it was announced in the *Gazette* that several persons, who were strongly suspected of being highwaymen, but against whom there was not sufficient evidence, would be paraded 15 at Newgate in riding dresses; their horses would also be shown; and all gentlemen who had been robbed were invited to inspect this singular exhibition. On another occasion a pardon was publicly offered to a robber if he would give up some rough diamonds of immense value which he had taken 20 when he stopped the Harwich mail. A short time after appeared another proclamation, warning the innkeepers that the eye of the government was upon them. Their criminal connivance, it was affirmed, enabled banditti to infest the roads with impunity. That these suspicions were not with- 25 out foundation is proved by the dying speeches of some penitent robbers of that age, who appear to have received from the innkeepers services much resembling those which Farquhar's Boniface rendered to Gibbet.[97]

It was necessary to the success and even to the safety of 30 the highwayman that he should be a bold and skillful rider, and that his manners and appearance should be such as suited the master of a fine horse. He therefore held an aristocratical position in the community of thieves, appeared at fashionable coffee-houses and gaming-houses, and betted with men of quality on the race-ground.* Sometimes, indeed, he was a man of good family and education. A romantic interest, therefore, attached, and perhaps still 5 attaches, to the names of freebooters of this class. The vulgar eagerly drank in tales of their ferocity and audacity, of their occasional acts of generosity and good-nature, of their amours, of their miraculous escapes, of their desperate struggles, and of their manly bearing at the bar and in the 10 cart. Thus it was related of William Nevison, the great robber of Yorkshire, that he levied a quarterly tribute on all the northern drovers, and in return, not only spared them himself, but protected them against all other thieves ; that he demanded purses in the most courteous manner ; that he 15 gave largely to the poor what he had taken from the rich ; that his life was once spared by the royal clemency, but that he again tempted his fate, and at length died, in 1685, on the gallows of York.† It was related how Claude Duval, the French page of the Duke of Richmond, took to the road, 20 became captain of a formidable gang, and had the honor to be named first in a royal proclamation against notorious offenders ; how at the head of his troop he stopped a lady's coach, in which there was a booty of four hundred pounds ; how he took only one hundred and suffered the fair owner 25 to ransom the rest by dancing a coranto with him on the

* *Aimwell.* Pray, sir, han't I seen your face at Will's coffee-house ?
Gibbet. Yes, sir, and at White's too. *Beaux' Stratagem.*

† Gent's *History of York.* Another marauder of the same description, named Biss, was hanged at Salisbury in 1695. In a ballad which 30 is in the Pepysian Library, he is represented as defending himself thus before the judge : —

> " What say you now, my honored Lord ?
> What harm was there in this ?
> Rich, wealthy misers were abhorred
35 > By brave, freehearted Biss."

heath ; how his vivacious gallantry stole away the hearts
of all women ; how his dexterity at sword and pistol made
him a terror to all men ; how at length, in the year 1670, he
was seized when overcome by wine ; how dames of high
rank visited him in prison, and with tears interceded for his 5
life ; how the king would have granted a pardon but for
the interference of Judge Morton, the terror of highwaymen,
who threatened to resign his office unless the law were
carried into full effect; and how, after the execution, the
corpse lay in state with all the pomp of scutcheons, wax 10
lights, black hangings, and mutes, till the same cruel judge
who had intercepted the mercy of the crown sent officers to
disturb the obsequies. In these anecdotes there is doubtless a large mixture of fable; but they are not on that
account unworthy of being recorded, for it is both an 15
authentic and an important fact that such tales, whether
false or true, were heard by our ancestors with eagerness
and faith.

All the various dangers by which the traveler was beset
were greatly increased by darkness. He was therefore com- 20
monly desirous of having the shelter of a roof during the
night, and such shelter it was not difficult to obtain. From
a very early period the inns of England had been renowned.
Our first great poet had described the excellent accommodation which they afforded to the pilgrims of the fourteenth 25
century. Nine and twenty persons, with their horses, found
room in the wide chambers and stables of the Tabard in
Southwark.[97a] The food was of the best, and the wines such
as drew the company on to drink largely. Two hundred
years later, under the reign of Elizabeth, William Harrison 30
gave a lively description of the plenty and comfort of the
great hostelries. The continent of Europe, he said, could
show nothing like them. There were some in which two or
three hundred people, with their horses, could without diffi-

culty be lodged and fed.   The bedding, the tapestry, above
all, the abundance of clean and fine linen was matter of
wonder.   Valuable plate was often set on the tables.   Nay,
there were signs which had cost thirty or forty pounds.   In
5 the seventeenth century England abounded with excellent
inns of every rank.   The traveler sometimes, in a small
village, lighted on a public house such as Walton has described, where the brick floor was swept clean, where the
walls were stuck round with ballads, where the sheets smelt
10 of lavender, and where a blazing fire, a cup of good ale, and
a dish of trouts fresh from the neighboring brook were to be
procured at small charge.   At the larger houses of entertainment were to be found beds hung with silk, choice cookery,
and claret equal to the best which was drunk in London.
15 The innkeepers too, it was said, were not like other innkeepers.   On the Continent the landlord was the tyrant of
those who crossed the threshold.   In England he was a
servant.   Never was an Englishman more at home than
when he took his ease in his inn.   Even men of fortune, who
20 might in their own mansions have enjoyed .every luxury,
were often in the habit of passing their evenings in the
parlor of some neighboring house of public entertainment.
They seem to have thought that comfort and freedom could
in no other place be enjoyed in equal perfection.   This
25 feeling continued during many generations to be a national
peculiarity.   The liberty and jollity of inns long furnished
matter to our novelists and dramatists.   Johnson declared
that a tavern chair was the throne of human felicity; and
Shenstone[98] gently complained that no private roof, however
30 friendly, gave the wanderer so warm a welcome as that
which was to be found at an inn.

Many conveniences, which were unknown at Hampton
Court and Whitehall in the seventeenth century, are to be
found in our modern hotels.   Yet on the whole it is certain

that the improvement of our houses of public entertainment has by no means kept pace with the improvement of our roads and of our conveyances. Nor is this strange ; for it is evident that, all other circumstances being supposed equal, the inns will be best where the means of locomotion are 5 worst. The quicker the rate of traveling, the less important is it that there should be numerous agreeable resting-places for the traveler. A hundred and sixty years ago, a person who came up to the capital from a remote county generally required twelve or fifteen meals and lodging for five or six 10 nights by the way. If he were a great man, he expected the meals and lodging to be comfortable and even luxurious. At present, we fly from York or Chester to London by the light of a single winter's day. At present, therefore, a traveler seldom interrupts his journey merely for the sake of 15 rest and refreshment. The consequence is that hundreds of excellent inns have fallen into utter decay. In a short time, no good houses of that description will be found, except at places where strangers are likely to be detained by business or pleasure. 20

The mode in which correspondence was carried on between distant places may excite the scorn of the present generation; yet it was such as might have moved the admiration and envy of the polished nations of antiquity or of the contemporaries of Raleigh and Cecil. A rude and imperfect 25 establishment of posts for the conveyance of letters had been set up by Charles the First, and had been swept away by the Civil War. Under the Commonwealth the design was resumed. At the Restoration the proceeds of the post office, after all expenses had been paid, were settled on the Duke 30 of York. On most lines of road the mails went out and came in only on the alternate days. In Cornwall, in the fens of Lincolnshire, and among the hills and lakes of Cumberland, letters were received only once a week. During a royal

progress a daily post was despatched from the capital to
the place where the court sojourned.   There was also daily
communication between London and the Downs; and the
same privilege was sometimes extended to Tunbridge Wells
5 and Bath at the seasons when those places were crowded by
the great.   The bags were carried on horseback day and
night, at the rate of about five miles an hour.

The revenue of this establishment was not derived solely
from the charge for the transmission of letters.   The post
10 office alone was entitled to furnish post horses; and from the
care with which this monopoly was guarded, we may infer
that it was found profitable.   If, indeed, a traveler had
waited half an hour without being supplied, he might hire a
horse wherever he could.

15   To facilitate correspondence between one part of London
and another was not originally one of the objects of the post
office.   But in the reign of Charles the Second, an enterprising citizen of London, William Dockwray, set up, at great
expense, a penny post, which delivered letters and parcels
20 six or eight times a day in the busy and crowded streets
near the Exchange, and four times a day in the outskirts of
the capital.   This improvement was, as usual, strenuously
resisted.   The porters complained that their interests were
attacked, and tore down the placards in which the scheme
25 was announced to the public.   The excitement caused by
Godfrey's death and by the discovery of Coleman's papers [99]
was then at the height.   A cry was therefore raised that the
penny post was a Popish contrivance.   The great Doctor
Oates,[100] it was affirmed, had hinted a suspicion that the
30 Jesuits were at the bottom of the scheme, and that the bags,
if examined, would be found full of treason.   The utility of
the enterprise was, however, so great and obvious that all
opposition proved fruitless.   As soon as it became clear that
the speculation would be lucrative, the Duke of York com-

plained of it as an infraction of his monopoly, and the courts
of law decided in his favor.

The revenue of the post office was from the first constantly
increasing. In the year of the Restoration a committee of
the House of Commons, after strict inquiry, had estimated 5
the net receipt at about twenty thousand pounds. At the
close of the reign of Charles the Second the net receipt was
little short of fifty thousand pounds, and this was then thought
a stupendous sum. The gross receipt was about seventy
thousand pounds. The charge for conveying a single letter 10
was twopence for eighty miles and threepence for a longer
distance. The postage increased in proportion to the weight
of the packet. At present a single letter is carried to the
extremity of Scotland or of Ireland for a penny, and the
monopoly of post horses has long ceased to exist. Yet 15
the gross annual receipts of the department amount to more
than £1,800,000, and the net receipts to more than £700,000.
It is, therefore, scarcely possible to doubt that the number
of letters now conveyed by mail is seventy times the number
which was so conveyed at the time of the accession of James 20
the Second.

No part of the load which the old mails carried out was
more important than the newsletters. In 1685 nothing like
the London daily paper of our time existed or could exist.
Neither the necessary capital nor the necessary skill was to 25
be found. Freedom, too, was wanting — a want as fatal as
that of either capital or skill. The press was not indeed at
that moment under a general censorship. The licensing act,
which had been passed soon after the Restoration, had
expired in 1679. Any person might, therefore, print, at his 30
own risk, a history, a sermon, or a poem, without the previous approbation of any public officer; but the judges were
unanimously of opinion that this liberty did not extend to
gazettes, and that, by the common law of England, no man,

not authorized by the crown, had a right to publish political news.   While the Whig party was still formidable, the government thought it expedient occasionally to connive at the violation of this rule.   During the great battle of the Exclu-
5 sion Bill, many newspapers were suffered to appear: the *Protestant Intelligence*, the *Current Intelligence*, the *Domestic Intelligence*, the *True News*, the London *Mercury*.   None of these were published oftener than twice a week.   None exceeded in size a single small leaf.   The quantity of matter
10 which one of them contained in a year was not more than is often found in two numbers of the *Times*.   After the defeat of the Whigs it was no longer necessary for the king to be sparing in the use of that which all his judges had pronounced to be his undoubted prerogative.   At the close of
15 his reign, no newspaper was suffered to appear without his allowance ; and his allowance was given exclusively to the London *Gazette*.   The London *Gazette* came out only on Mondays and Thursdays.   The contents generally were a royal proclamation, two or three Tory addresses, notices of
20 two or three promotions, an account of a skirmish between the imperial troops and the Janizaries [101] on the Danube, a description of a highwayman, an announcement of a grand cockfight between two persons of honor, and an advertisement offering a reward for a strayed dog.   The whole made
25 up two pages of moderate size.   Whatever was communicated respecting matters of the highest moment was communicated in the most meagre and formal style.   Sometimes, indeed, when the government was disposed to gratify the public curiosity respecting an important transaction, a broad-
30 side was put forth, giving fuller details than could be found in the *Gazette;* but neither the *Gazette* nor any supplementary broadside printed by authority ever contained any intelligence which it did not suit the purposes of the court to publish.   The most important parliamentary debates, the

most important state trials recorded in our history were passed over in profound silence.*   In the capital the coffee-houses supplied, in some measure, the place of a journal. Thither the Londoners flocked as the Athenians of old flocked to the market-place to hear whether there was any 5 news.   There men might learn how brutally a Whig had been treated the day before in Westminster Hall, what horrible accounts the letters from Edinburgh gave of the torturing of Covenanters, how grossly the navy board had cheated the crown in the victualling of the fleet, and what 10 grave charges the Lord Privy Seal had brought against the treasury in the matter of the hearth money.   But people who lived at a distance from the great theatre of political contention could be kept regularly informed of what was passing there only by means of newsletters.   To prepare 15 such letters became a calling in London, as it now is among the natives of India.   The newswriter rambled from coffee-room to coffee-room, collecting reports, squeezed himself into the Sessions House at the Old Bailey, if there was an interesting trial, nay, perhaps obtained admission to the gallery 20 of Whitehall, and noticed how the king and duke looked. In this way he gathered materials for weekly epistles, destined to enlighten some country town or some bench of rustic magistrates.   Such were the sources from which the inhabitants of the largest provincial cities and the great 25 body of the gentry and clergy learned almost all that they knew of the history of their own time.   We must suppose that at Cambridge there were as many persons curious to know what was passing in the world as at almost any place in the kingdom, out of London.   Yet at Cambridge, during 30 a great part of the reign of Charles the Second, the doctors

---

* For example, there is not a word in the *Gazette* about the important parliamentary proceedings of November, 1685, or about the trial and acquittal of the seven bishops.

of laws and the masters of arts had no regular supply of
news except through the London *Gazette.* At length the services of one of the collectors of intelligence in the capital
were employed. That was a memorable day on which the
5 first newsletter from London was laid on the table of the
only coffee-room in Cambridge. At the seat of a man of
fortune in the country, the newsletter was impatiently
expected. Within a week after it had arrived, it had been
thumbed by twenty families. It furnished the neighboring
10 squires with matter for talk over their October, and the neighboring rectors with topics for sharp sermons against Whig-
gery or Popery. Many of these curious journals might
doubtless still be detected by a diligent search in the archives
of old families. Some are to be found in our public libraries;
15 and one series, which is not the least valuable part of the
literary treasures collected by Sir James Mackintosh, will be
occasionally quoted in the course of this work.

It is scarcely necessary to say that there were then no
provincial newspapers. Indeed, except in the capital and
20 at the two universities, there was scarcely a printer in the
kingdom. The only press in England north of Trent appears to have been at York.

It was not only by means of the London *Gazette* that the
government undertook to furnish political instruction to the
25 people. That journal contained a scanty supply of news
without comment. Another journal, published under the
patronage of the court, consisted of comment without news.
This paper, called the *Observator,* was edited by an old
Tory pamphleteer named Roger Lestrange. Lestrange was
30 by no means deficient in readiness and shrewdness, and
his diction, though coarse and disfigured by a mean and
flippant jargon which then passed for wit in the greenroom
and the tavern, was not without keenness and vigor. But
his nature, at once ferocious and ignoble, showed itself in

every line that he penned.   When the first *Observators*
appeared, there was some excuse for his acrimony.   For
the Whigs were then powerful, and he had to contend
against numerous adversaries, whose unscrupulous violence
might seem to justify unsparing retaliation.   But in 1685   5
all opposition had been crushed.   A generous spirit would
have disdained to insult a party which could not reply, and
to aggravate the misery of prisoners, of exiles, of bereaved
families ; but from the malice of Lestrange the grave was
no hiding-place and the house of mourning no sanctuary.   10
In the last month of the reign of Charles the Second, William Jenkyn, an aged dissenting pastor of great note, who
had been cruelly persecuted for no crime but that of wor-
shipping God according to the fashion generally followed
throughout Protestant Europe, died of hardships and priva-   15
tions in Newgate.   The outbreak of popular sympathy could
not be repressed.   The corpse was followed to the grave
by a train of a hundred and fifty coaches.   Even courtiers
looked sad.   Even the unthinking king showed some signs
of concern.   Lestrange alone set up a howl of savage ex-   20
ultation, laughed at the weak compassion of the Trimmers,
proclaimed that the blasphemous old impostor had met with
a most righteous punishment, and vowed to wage war, not
only to the death, but after death, with all the mock saints
and martyrs.   Such was the spirit of the paper which was   25
at this time the oracle of the Tory party, and especially of
the parochial clergy.

Literature which could be carried by the post bag then
formed the greater part of the intellectual nutriment rumi-
nated by the country divines and country justices.   The   30
difficulty and expense of conveying large packets from place
to place were so great that an extensive work was longer
in making its way from Paternoster Row to Devonshire or
Lancashire than it now is in reaching Kentucky.   How

scantily a rural parsonage was then furnished, even with
books the most necessary to a theologian, has already been
remarked. The houses of the gentry were not more plenti-
fully supplied. Few knights of the shire had libraries so
5 good as may now perpetually be found in a servant's hall
or in the back parlor of a small shopkeeper. An esquire
passed among his neighbors for a great scholar if *Hudibras*
and *Baker's Chronicle, Tarlton's Jests*, and the *Seven Champions of Christendom* lay in his hall window among the fish-
10 ing-rods and fowling-pieces. No circulating library, no book
society then existed even in the capital; but in the capital
those students who could not afford to purchase largely
had a resource. The shops of the great booksellers, near
Saint Paul's Churchyard, were crowded every day and all
15 day long with readers, and a known customer was often
permitted to carry a volume home. In the country there
was no such accommodation, and every man was under the
necessity of buying whatever he wished to read.*

As to the lady of the manor and her daughters, their
20 literary stores generally consisted of a prayer book and a
receipt book. But in truth they lost little by living in rural
seclusion. For even in the highest ranks and in those
situations which afforded the greatest facilities for mental
improvement, the English women of that generation were
25 decidedly worse educated than they have been at any other
time since the Revival of Learning. At an earlier period,
they had studied the masterpieces of ancient genius. In
the present day, they seldom bestow much attention on the
dead languages, but they are familiar with the tongue of

30   * Cotton seems, from his *Angler*, to have found room for his whole
library in his hall window, and Cotton was a man of letters. Even
when Franklin first visited London in 1724, circulating libraries were
unknown there. The crowd at the booksellers' shops in Little Britain
is mentioned by Roger North in his life of his brother John.

Pascal and Molière,[102] with the tongue of Dante and
Tasso,[103] with the tongue of Goethe and Schiller;[104] nor is
there any purer or more graceful English than that which
accomplished women now speak and write. But during the
latter part of the seventeenth century, the culture of the 5
female mind seems to have been almost entirely neglected.
If a damsel had the least smattering of literature, she was
regarded as a prodigy. Ladies highly born, highly bred,
and naturally quick-witted were unable to write a line in
their mother tongue without solecisms and faults of spelling 10
such as a charity girl would now be ashamed to commit.*
The explanation may easily be found. Extravagant licentiousness, the natural effect of extravagant austerity, was
now the mode; and licentiousness had produced its ordinary
effect, the moral and intellectual degradation of women. 15
To their personal beauty it was the fashion to pay rude and
impudent homage. But the admiration and desire which
they inspired were seldom mingled with respect, with affection, or with any chivalrous sentiment. The qualities which
fit them to be companions, advisers, confidential friends, 20
rather repelled than attracted the libertines of Whitehall.
In that court, a maid of honor, who dressed in such a manner as to do full justice to a white bosom, who ogled signi-
ficantly, who danced voluptuously, who excelled in pert
repartee, who was not ashamed to romp with lords of the 25
bedchamber and captains of the guards, to sing sly verses
with sly expression, or to put on a page's dress for a frolic,
was more likely to be followed and admired, more likely to

* One instance will suffice. Queen Mary had good natural abilities.
had been educated by a bishop, was fond of history and poetry, and 30
was regarded by very eminent men as a superior woman. There is, in
the library of the Hague, a superb English Bible which was delivered
to her when she was crowned in Westminister Abbey. In the title
page are these words in her own hand: "This book was given the
king and I, at our crownation. Marie R." 35

be honored with royal attentions, more likely to win a rich
and noble husband than Jane Grey or Lucy Hutchinson
would have been.[105]   In such circumstances the standard of
female attainments was necessarily low ; and it was more
5 dangerous to be above that standard than to be beneath it.
Extreme ignorance and frivolity were thought less unbecom-
ing in a lady than the slightest tincture of pedantry.   Of
the too celebrated women whose faces we still admire on
the walls of Hampton Court, few indeed were in the habit
10 of reading anything more valuable than acrostics, lampoons,
and translations of the *Clelia* and the *Grand Cyrus*.[106]

The literary acquirements, even of the accomplished gentlemen of that generation, seem to have been somewhat less
solid and profound than at an earlier or a later period.
15 Greek learning, at least, did not flourish among us in the
days of Charles the Second as it had flourished before the
Civil War, or as it again flourished long after the Revolution.   There were undoubtedly scholars to whom the whole
Greek literature from Homer to Photius was familiar ; but
20 such scholars were to be found almost exclusively among
the clergy resident at the universities, and even at the universities were few, and were not fully appreciated.   At
Cambridge it was not thought by any means necessary that
a divine should be able to read the Gospels in the original.*
25 Nor was the standard at Oxford higher.   When, in the reign
of William the Third, Christ Church rose up as one man to
defend the genuineness of the Epistles of Phalaris,[107] that
great college, then considered as the first seat of philology in
the kingdom, could not muster such a stock of Attic learn-
30 ing as is now possessed by several youths at every great
public school.   It may easily be supposed that a dead lan-

---

* Roger North tells us that his brother John, who was Greek professor at Cambridge, complained bitterly of the general neglect of the
Greek tongue among the academical clergy.

guage, neglected at the universities, was not much studied by men of the world. In a former age, the poetry and eloquence of Greece had been the delight of Raleigh and Falkland.[108] In a later age, the poetry and eloquence of Greece were the delight of Pitt and Fox, of Windham and 5 Grenville.[109] But during the latter part of the seventeenth century there was in England scarcely one eminent statesman who could read with enjoyment a page of Sophocles or Plato.

Good Latin scholars were numerous. The language of 10 Rome, indeed, had not altogether lost its imperial character, and was still, in many parts of Europe, almost indispensable to a traveler or a negotiator. To speak it well was therefore a much more common accomplishment than in our time ; and neither Oxford nor Cambridge wanted poets who, 15 on a great occasion, could lay at the foot of the throne happy imitations of the verses in which Virgil and Ovid had celebrated the greatness of Augustus.[110]

Yet even the Latin was giving way to a younger rival. France united at that time almost every species of ascend- 20 ency. Her military glory was at the height. She had vanquished mighty coalitions. She had dictated treaties. She had subjugated great cities and provinces. She had forced the Castilian pride to yield her the precedence. She had summoned Italian princes to prostrate themselves at 25 her footstool. Her authority was supreme in all matters of good breeding, from a duel to a minuet. She determined how a gentleman's coat must be cut, how long his peruke must be, whether his heels must be high or low, and whether the lace on his hat must be broad or narrow. In literature 30 she gave law to the world. The fame of her great writers filled Europe. No other country could produce a tragic poet equal to Racine,[111] a comic poet equal to Molière, a trifler so agreeable as La Fontaine,[112] a rhetorician so skillful

as Bossuet. The literary glory of Italy and of Spain had set ;
that of Germany had not yet dawned.   The genius, therefore, of the eminent men who adorned Paris shone forth
with a splendor which was set off to full advantage by con-
5 trast.   France, indeed, had at that time an empire over
mankind, such as even the Roman Republic never attained.
For when Rome was politically dominant, she was in arts
and letters the humble pupil of Greece.   France had, over
the surrounding countries, at once the ascendency which
10 Rome had over Greece, and the ascendency which Greece
had over Rome.   French was fast becoming the universal
language, the language of fashionable society, the language
of diplomacy.   At several courts princes and nobles spoke
it more accurately and politely than their mother tongue.
15 In our island there was less of this servility than on the
Continent.   Neither our good nor our bad qualities were
those of imitators.   Yet even here homage was paid, awk-
wardly indeed and sullenly, to the literary supremacy of our
neighbors.   The melodious Tuscan, so familiar to the gal-
20 lants and ladies of the court of Elizabeth, sank into contempt.   A gentleman who quoted Horace or Terence was
considered in good company as a pompous pedant.   But to
garnish his conversation with scraps of French was the best
proof which he could give of his parts and attainments.*
25 New canons of criticism, new models of style came into
fashion.   The quaint ingenuity which had deformed the
verses of Donne [113] and had been a blemish on those of
Cowley [114] disappeared from our poetry.   Our prose became
less majestic, less artfully involved, less variously musical

30   * Butler in a satire of great asperity says,

> " For, though to smatter words of Greek
> And Latin be the rhetorique
> Of pedants counted, and vainglorious,
> To smatter French is meritorious."

than that of an earlier age, but more lucid, more easy, and
better fitted for controversy and narrative.   In these changes
it is impossible not to recognize the influence of French
precept and of French example.   Great masters of our language, in their most dignified compositions, affected to use 5
French words when English words, quite as expressive and
melodious, were at hand : * and from France was imported
the tragedy in rhyme, an exotic which, in our soil, drooped
and speedily died.

It would have been well if our writers had also copied the 10
decorum which their great French contemporaries, with few
exceptions, preserved; for the profligacy of the English
plays, satires, songs, and novels of that age is a deep blot
on our national fame.   The evil may easily be traced to its
source.   The wits and the Puritans had never been on 15
friendly terms.   There was no sympathy between the two
classes.   They looked on the whole system of human life
from different points and in different lights.   The earnest of
each was the jest of the other.   The pleasures of each were
the torments of the other.   To the stern precisian even the 20
innocent sport of the fancy seemed a crime.   To light and
festive natures the solemnity of the zealous brethren furnished copious matter of ridicule.   From the Reformation
to the Civil War, almost every writer, gifted with a fine
sense of the ludicrous, had taken some opportunity of assail- 25
ing the straight-haired, snuffling, whining saints, who chris-
tened their children out of the Book of Nehemiah, who
groaned in spirit at the sight of Jack in the Green,[115] and
who thought it impious to taste plum porridge on Christmas

* The most offensive instance which I remember is in a poem on 30
the coronation of Charles the Second by Dryden, who certainly could
not plead poverty as an excuse for borrowing words from any foreign
tongue :   " Hither in summer evenings you repair,
          To taste the fraicheur of the cooler air."

Day.   At length a time came when the laughers began to
look grave in their turn.   The rigid, ungainly zealots, after
having furnished much good sport during two generations,
rose up in arms, conquered, ruled, and, grimly smiling, trod
5 down under their feet the whole crowd of mockers.   The
wounds inflicted by gay and petulant malice were retaliated
with the gloomy and implacable malice peculiar to bigots
who mistake their own rancor for virtue.   The theatres
were closed.   The players were flogged.   The press was
10 put under the guardianship of austere licensers.   The Muses
were banished from their own favorite haunts.   Cowley was
ejected from Cambridge and Crashaw from Oxford.[116]   The
young candidate for academical honors was no longer required to write Ovidian epistles or Virgilian pastorals, but
15 was strictly interrogated by a synod of lowering Supralapsarians[117] as to the day and hour when he experienced the
new birth.   Such a system was of course fruitful of hypo-
crites.   Under sober clothing and under visages composed
to the expression of austerity lay hid during several years
20 the intense desire of license and of revenge.   At length
that desire was gratified.   The Restoration emancipated
thousands of minds from a yoke which had become insupportable.   The old fight recommenced, but with an ani-
mosity altogether new.   It was now not a sportive combat,
25 but a war to the death.   The Roundhead had no better
quarter to expect from those whom he had persecuted than
a cruel slave-driver can expect from insurgent slaves still
bearing the marks of his collars and his scourges.

The war between wit and Puritanism soon became a war
30 between wit and morality.   The hostility excited by a grotesque caricature of virtue did not spare virtue herself.
Whatever the canting Roundhead had regarded with reverence was insulted.   Whatever he had proscribed was favored.   Because he had been scrupulous about trifles, all

scruples were treated with derision. Because he had covered his failings with the mask of devotion, men were en-
couraged to obtrude with cynic impudence all their most
scandalous vices on the public eye. Because he had pun-
ished illicit love with barbarous severity, virgin purity and 5
conjugal fidelity were to be made a jest. To that sancti-
monious jargon, which was his shibboleth, was opposed
another jargon not less absurd and much more odious. As
he never opened his mouth except in Scriptural phrase, the
new breed of wits and fine gentlemen never opened their 10
mouths without uttering ribaldry of which a porter would
now be ashamed, and without calling on their Maker to
curse them, sink them, confound them, blast them, and
damn them.

It is not strange, therefore, that our polite literature, 15
when it revived with the revival of the old civil and ecclesiastical polity, should have been profoundly immoral. A
few eminent men, who belonged to an earlier and better
age, were exempt from the general contagion. The verse
of Waller[118] still breathed the sentiments which had ani- 20
mated a more chivalrous generation. Cowley, distinguished
at once as a loyalist and as a man of letters, raised his
voice courageously against the immorality which disgraced
both letters and loyalty. A mightier spirit, unsubdued
by pain, danger, poverty, obloquy, and blindness, medi- 25
tated, undisturbed by the obscene tumult which raged all
around, a song so sublime and so holy that it would not
have misbecome the lips of those ethereal Virtues whom he
saw, what that inner eye which no calamity could darken,
flinging down on the jasper pavement their crowns of 30
amaranth and gold.[118a] The vigorous and fertile genius of
Butler,[119] if it did not altogether escape the prevailing infection, took the disease in a mild form. But these were men
whose minds had been trained in a world which had passed

away. They gave place in no long time to a younger generation of poets, and of that generation, from Dryden down
to Durfey, the common characteristic was hard-hearted,
shameless, swaggering licentiousness, at once inelegant and
5 inhuman. The influence of these writers was doubtless
noxious, yet less noxious than it would have been had they
been less depraved. The poison which they administered
was so strong that it was, in no long time, rejected with
nausea. None of them understood the dangerous art of
10 associating images of unlawful pleasure with all that is en-
dearing and ennobling. None of them was aware that a
certain decorum is essential even to voluptuousness, that
drapery may be more alluring than exposure, and that the
imagination may be far more powerfully moved by delicate
15 hints which impel it to exert itself than by gross descriptions which it takes in passively.

The spirit of the Anti-Puritan reaction pervades almost
the whole polite literature of the reign of Charles the
Second. But the very quintessence of that spirit will be
20 found in the comic drama. The playhouses, shut by the
meddling fanatic in the day of his power, were again
crowded. To their old attractions new and more powerful
attractions had been added. Scenery, dresses, and decorations such as would now be thought mean and absurd, but
25 such as would have been esteemed incredibly magnificent
by those who, early in the seventeenth century, sate on the
filthy benches of the Hope or under the thatched roof of
the Rose, dazzled the eyes of the multitude. The fascination of sex was called in to aid the fascination of art; and
30 the young spectator saw, with emotions unknown to the
contemporaries of Shakespeare and Jonson,[120] tender and
sprightly heroines personified by lovely women.[121] From
the day on which the theatres were reopened they became
seminaries of vice, and the evil propagated itself. The

profligacy of the representations soon drove away sober people. The frivolous and dissolute who remained required every year stronger and stronger stimulants. Thus the artists corrupted the spectators, and the spectators the artists, till the turpitude of the drama became such as must 5 astonish all who are not aware that extreme relaxation is the natural effect of extreme restraint, and that an age of hypocrisy is, in the regular course of things, followed by an age of impudence.

Nothing is more characteristic of the times than the care 10 with which the poets contrived to put all their loosest verses into the mouths of women. The compositions in which the greatest license was taken were the epilogues. They were almost always recited by favorite actresses, and nothing charmed the depraved audience so much as to hear lines 15 grossly indecent repeated by a beautiful girl, who was supposed to have not yet lost her innocence.

Our theatre was indebted in that age for many plots and characters to Spain, to France, and to the old English masters; but whatever our dramatists touched they tainted. In 20 their imitations the houses of Calderon's [122] stately and high spirited Castilian gentlemen became sties of vice, Shakespeare's Viola [123] a procuress, Molière's misanthrope a ravisher, Molière's Agnes an adulteress. Nothing could be so pure or so heroic but that it became foul and ignoble by 25 transfusion through those foul and ignoble minds.

Such was the state of the drama ; and the drama was the department of light literature in which a poet had the best chance of obtaining a subsistence by his pen. The sale of books was so small that a man of the greatest name could 30 expect only a pittance for the copyright of the best performance. There cannot be a stronger instance than the fate of Dryden's last production, the *Fables*. That volume was published when he was universally admitted to be

the chief of living English poets. It contains about twelve
thousand lines. The versification is admirable, the narratives and descriptions full of life. To this day *Palamon
and Arcite, Cymon and Iphigenia, Theodore and Honoria*
5 are the delight both of critics and of schoolboys. The
collection includes *Alexander's Feast*, the noblest ode in our
language. For the copyright Dryden received two hundred
and fifty pounds, less than in our days has sometimes been
paid for two articles in a review. Nor does the bargain
10 seem to have been a hard one. For the book went off
slowly, and a second edition was not required till the
author had been ten years in his grave. By writing for the
theatre it was possible to earn a much larger sum with
much less trouble. Southern [124] made seven hundred
15 pounds by one play. Otway [125] was raised from beggary to
temporary affluence by the success of his *Don Carlos.*
Shadwell [126] cleared a hundred and thirty pounds by a single
representation of the *Squire of Alsatia.* The consequence
was that every man who had to live by his wit wrote plays
20 whether he had any internal vocation to write plays or not.
It was thus with Dryden. As a satirist he has rivaled
Juvenal.[127] As a didactic poet he perhaps might, with care
and meditation, have rivaled Lucretius.[128] Of lyric poets
he is, if not the most sublime, the most brilliant and spirit-
25 stirring. But nature, profuse to him of many rare gifts,
had denied him the dramatic faculty. Nevertheless all the
energies of his best years were wasted on dramatic com-
position. He had too much judgment not to be aware that
in the power of exhibiting character by means of dialogue
30 he was deficient. That deficiency he did his best to con-
ceal, sometimes by surprising and amusing incidents, sometimes by stately declamation, sometimes by harmonious
numbers, sometimes by ribaldry but too well suited to the
taste of a profane and licentious pit. Yet he never ob-

tained any theatrical success equal to that which rewarded
the exertions of some men far inferior to him in general
powers.   He thought himself fortunate if he cleared a hundred guineas by a play ; a scanty remuneration, yet appar-
ently larger than he could have earned in any other way 5
by the same quantity of labor.

The recompense which the wits of that age could obtain
from the public was so small that they were under the
necessity of eking out their incomes by levying contribu-
tions on the great.   Every rich and good-natured lord was 10
pestered by authors with a mendicancy so importune, and a
flattery so abject, as may in our time seem incredible.   The
patron to whom a work was inscribed was expected to reward the writer with a purse of gold.   The fee paid for the
dedication of a book was often much larger than the sum 15
which any bookseller would give for the copyright.   Books
were therefore often printed merely that they might be
dedicated.   This traffic in praise completed the degradation of the literary character.   Adulation pushed to the
verge, sometimes of nonsense and sometimes of impiety, 20
was not thought to disgrace a poet.   Independence, verac-
ity, self-respect, were things not expected by the world
from him.   In truth, he was in morals something between a
pandar and a beggar.

To the other vices which degraded the literary character 25
was added, toward the close of the reign of Charles the
Second, the most savage intemperance of party spirit.   The
wits, as a class, had been impelled by their old hatred of
Puritanism to take the side of the court, and had been
found useful allies.   Dryden, in particular, had done good 30
service to the government.   His *Absalom and Achitophel*,
the greatest satire of modern times, had amazed the town,
had made its way with unprecedented rapidity even into
rural districts, and had, wherever it appeared, bitterly an-

noyed the Exclusionists and raised the courage of the Tories. But we must not, in the admiration which we naturally feel for noble diction and versification, forget the great distinctions of good and evil. The spirit by which
5 Dryden and several of his compeers were at this time animated against the Whigs deserves to be called fiendish. The servile judges and sheriffs of those evil days could not shed blood so fast as the poets cried out for it. Calls for more victims, hideous jests on hanging, bitter taunts on
10 those who, having stood by the king in the hour of danger, now advised him to deal mercifully and generously by his vanquished enemies, were publicly recited on the stage, and, that nothing might be wanting to the guilt and the shame, were recited by women, who, having long been
15 taught to discard all modesty, were now taught to discard all compassion.

It is a remarkable fact that, while the lighter literature of England was thus becoming a nuisance and a national disgrace, the English genius was effecting in science a revolution
20 which will, to the end of time, be reckoned among the highest achievements of the human intellect. Bacon had sown the good seed in a sluggish soil and an ungenial season. He had not expected an early crop, and in his last testament had solemnly bequeathed his fame to the next age. During
25 a whole generation his philosophy had, amidst tumults, wars, and proscriptions, been slowly ripening in a few well-constituted minds. While factions were struggling for dominion over each other, a small body of sages had turned away with benevolent disdain from the conflict, and had devoted them-
30 selves to the nobler work of extending the dominion of man over matter. As soon as tranquillity was restored, these teachers easily found attentive audience. For the discipline through which the nation had passed had brought the public mind to a temper well fitted for the reception of the Veru-

lamian doctrine.[129]   The civil troubles had stimulated the
faculties of the educated classes and had called forth a
restless activity and an insatiable curiosity such as had not
before been known among us.   Yet the effect of those
troubles had been that schemes of political and religious 5
reform were generally regarded with suspicion and contempt.
During twenty years the chief employment of busy and
ingenious men had been to frame constitutions with first
magistrates, without first magistrates, with hereditary senates,
with senates appointed by lot, with annual senates, with per- 10
petual senates.   In these plans nothing was omitted.   All
the detail, all the nomenclature, all the ceremonial of the
imaginary government was fully set forth — Polemarchs and
Phylarchs, Tribes and Galaxies, the Lord Archon and the
Lord Strategus.   Which ballot boxes were to be green and 15
which red, which balls were to be of gold and which of
silver, which magistrates were to wear hats and which black
velvet caps with peaks, how the mace was to be carried and
when the heralds were to uncover, — these and a hundred
more such trifles were gravely considered and arranged by 20
men of no common capacity and learning.   But the time for
these visions had gone by; and, if any steadfast republican
still continued to amuse himself with them, fear of public
derision and of a criminal information generally induced him
to keep his fancies to himself.   It was now unpopular and 25
unsafe to mutter a word against the fundamental laws of the
monarchy; but daring and ingenious men might indemnify
themselves by treating with disdain what had lately been
considered as the fundamental laws of nature.   The torrent
which had been dammed up in one channel rushed violently 30
into another.   The revolutionary spirit, ceasing to operate in
politics, began to exert itself with unprecedented vigor and
hardihood in every department of physics.   The year 1660,
the era of the restoration of the old constitution, is also the

era from which dates the ascendency of the new philosophy. In that year the Royal Society, destined to be a chief agent in a long series of glorious and salutary reforms, began to exist.   In a few months experimental science became all
5 the mode.   The transfusion of blood, the ponderation of air, the fixation of mercury, succeeded to that place in the public mind which had been lately occupied by the controversies of the Rota.   Dreams of perfect forms of government made way for dreams of wings with which men were to fly from the
10 Tower to the Abbey, and of double-keeled ships which were never to founder in the fiercest storm.   All classes were hurried along by the prevailing sentiment.   Cavalier and Roundhead, Churchman and Puritan were for once allied. Divines, jurists, statesmen, nobles, princes swelled the tri-
15 umph of the Baconian philosophy.   Poets sang with emulous fervor the approach of the golden age.   Cowley, in lines weighty with thought and resplendent with wit, urged the chosen seed to take possession of the promised land flowing with milk and honey, that land which their great deliverer
20 and lawgiver had seen as from the summit of Pisgah, but had not been permitted to enter.   Dryden, with more zeal than knowledge, joined his voice to the general acclamation, and foretold things which neither he nor anybody else understood.   The Royal Society, he predicted, would soon
25 lead us to the extreme verge of the globe, and there delight us with a better view of the moon.*   Two able and aspiring prelates, Ward, Bishop of Salisbury, and Wilkins, Bishop of Chester, were conspicuous among the leaders of the movement.   Its history was eloquently written by a younger

30   * " Then we upon the globe's last verge shall go,
And view the ocean leaning on the sky;
From thence our rolling neighbors we shall know,
And on the lunar world securely pry."

Annus Mirabilis, 164.

divine who was rising to high distinction in his profession, Thomas Sprat, afterwards Bishop of Rochester. Both Chief Justice Hale and Lord Keeper Guildford stole some hours from the business of their courts to write on hydrostatics. Indeed it was under the immediate directions of Guildford 5 that the first barometers ever exposed to sale in London were constructed. Chemistry divided, for a time, with wine and love, with the stage and the gaming-table, with the intrigues of a courtier and the intrigues of a demagogue, the attention of the fickle Buckingham. Rupert[130] has the credit 10 of having invented mezzotinto, and from him is named that curious bubble of glass which has long amused children and puzzled philosophers. Charles himself had a laboratory at Whitehall, and was far more active and attentive there than at the council board. It was almost necessary to the char- 15 acter of a fine gentleman to have something to say about air-pumps and telescopes; and even fine ladies, now and then, thought it becoming to affect a taste for science, went in coaches and six to visit the Gresham curiosities, and broke forth into cries of delight at finding that a magnet really 20 attracted a needle, and that a microscope really made a fly look as large as a sparrow.

In this, as in every great stir of the human mind, there was doubtless something which might well move a smile. It is the universal law that whatever pursuit, whatever doctrine 25 becomes fashionable shall lose a portion of that dignity which it had possessed while it was confined to a small but earnest minority, and was loved for its own sake alone. It is true that the follies of some persons who, without any real aptitude for science, professed a passion for it, furnished matter of 30 contemptuous mirth to a few malignant satirists who belonged to the preceding generation, and were not disposed to unlearn the lore of their youth. But it is not less true that the great work of interpreting nature was performed by the English of

that age as it had never before been performed in any age
by any nation.   The spirit of Francis Bacon was abroad, a
spirit admirably compounded of audacity and sobriety.   There
was a strong persuasion that the whole world was full of
5 secrets of high moment to the happiness of man, and that
man had, by his Maker, been intrusted with the key which,
rightly used, would give access to them.   There was at the
same time a conviction that in physics it was impossible to
arrive at the knowledge of general laws except by the care-
10 ful observation of particular facts.   Deeply impressed with
these great truths, the professors of the new philosophy
applied themselves to their task, and before a quarter of a
century had expired, they had given ample earnest of what
has since been achieved.   Already a reform of agriculture
15 had been commenced.   New vegetables were cultivated.
New implements of husbandry were employed.   New man-
ures were applied to the soil.   Evelyn[131] had, under the
formal sanction of the Royal Society, given instruction to
his countrymen in planting.   Temple, in his intervals of
20 leisure, had tried many experiments in horticulture, and had
proved that many delicate fruits, the natives of more favored
climates, might, with the help of art, be grown on English
ground.   Medicine, which in France was still in abject bond-
age and afforded an inexhaustible subject of just ridicule
25 to Molière, had in England become an experimental and
progressive science, and every day made some new advance,
in defiance of Hippocrates and Galen.[132]   The attention of
speculative men had been, for the first time, directed to the
important subject of sanitary police.   The great plague of
30 1665 induced them to consider with care the defective architecture, draining, and ventilation of the capital.   The great
fire of 1666 afforded an opportunity for effecting extensive
improvements.   The whole matter was diligently examined
by the Royal Society, and to the suggestions of that body

must be partly attributed the changes which, though far short of what the public welfare required, yet made a wide difference between the new and the old London, and probably put a final close to the ravages of pestilence in our country. At the same time one of the founders of the society, Sir William Petty, created the science of political arithmetic, the humble but indispensable handmaid of political philosophy. To that period belonged the chemical discoveries of Boyle and the first botanical researches of Sloane.[133] One after another, phantoms which had haunted the world through ages of darkness fled before the light. Astrology and alchemy became jests. Soon there was scarcely a county in which some of the quorum did not smile contemptuously when an old woman was brought before them for riding on broomsticks or giving cattle the murrain. But it was in those noblest and most arduous departments of knowledge in which induction and mathematical demonstration coöperate for the discovery of truth that the English genius won in that age the most memorable triumphs. John Wallis placed the whole system of statics on a new foundation. Edmund Halley investigated the properties of the atmosphere, the ebb and flow of the sea, the laws of magnetism, and the course of the comets ; nor did he shrink from toil, peril, and exile in the cause of science. While he, on the rock of St. Helena, mapped the constellations of the southern hemisphere, our national observatory was rising at Greenwich ; and John Flamsteed, the first astronomer royal, was commencing that long series of observations which is never mentioned without respect and gratitude in any part of the globe. But the glory of these men, eminent as they were, is cast into the shade by the transcendent luster of one immortal name. In Isaac Newton two kinds of intellectual power which have little in common and which are not often found together in a very

high degree of vigor, but which nevertheless are equally
necessary in the most sublime departments of natural philosophy, were united as they have never been united before
or since. There may have been minds as happily constituted
5 as his for the cultivation of pure mathematical science; there
may have been minds as happily constituted for the cultivation of science purely experimental; but in no other mind
have the demonstrative faculty and the inductive faculty
coexisted in such supreme excellence and perfect harmony.
10 Perhaps in an age of Scotists and Thomists [134] even his
intellect might have run to waste, as many intellects ran to
waste which were inferior only to his. Happily the spirit of
the age on which his lot was cast gave the right direction to
his mind; and his mind reacted with tenfold force on the
15 spirit of the age. In the year 1685 his fame, though splen
did, was only dawning; but his genius was in the meridian.
His great work, that work which effected a revolution in the
most important provinces of natural philosophy, had been
completed, but was not yet published, and was just about to
20 be submitted to the consideration of the Royal Society.

It is not very easy to explain why the nation which was so
far before its neighbors in science should in art have been
far behind them all. Yet such was the fact. It is true that
in architecture, an art which is half a science, an art in which
25 none but a geometrician can excel, an art which has no
standard of grace but what is directly or indirectly dependent
on utility, an art of which the creations derive a part, at least,
of their majesty from mere bulk, our country could boast of
one truly great man, Christopher Wren; [135] and the fire which
30 laid London in ruins had given him an opportunity, unprecedented in modern history, of displaying his powers. The
austere beauty of the Athenian portico, the gloomy sublimity
of the Gothic arcade, he was, like almost all his contemporaries, incapable of emulating, and perhaps incapable of

appreciating; but no man, born on our side of the Alps, has imitated with so much success the magnificence of the palace-like churches of Italy. Even the superb Louis [186] has left to posterity no work which can bear a comparison with Saint Paul's. But at the close of the reign of Charles the Second there was not a single English painter or statuary whose name is now remembered. This sterility is somewhat mysterious, for painters and statuaries were by no means a despised or an ill-paid class. Their social position was at least as high as at present. Their gains, when compared with the wealth of the nation and with the remuneration of other descriptions of intellectual labor, were even larger than at present. Indeed, the munificent patronage which was extended to artists drew them to our shores in multitudes. Lely,[187] who has preserved to us the rich curls, the full lips, and the languishing eyes of the frail beauties celebrated by Hamilton,[188] was a Westphalian. He had died in 1680, having long lived splendidly, having received the honor of knighthood, and having accumulated a good estate out of the fruits of his skill. His noble collection of drawings and pictures was, after his decease, exhibited by the royal permission in the Banqueting House at Whitehall, and sold by auction for the almost incredible sum of twenty-six thousand pounds, a sum which bore a greater proportion to the fortunes of the rich men of that day than a hundred thousand pounds would bear to the fortunes of the rich men of our time. Lely was succeeded by his countryman Godfrey Kneller,[189] who was made first a knight and then a baronet, and who, after keeping up a sumptuous establishment, and after losing much money by unlucky speculations, was still able to bequeath a large fortune to his family. The two Vandeveldes, natives of Holland, had been induced by English liberality to settle here, and had produced for the king and his nobles some of the finest sea-pieces in the world. Another Dutchman,

Simon Varelst, painted glorious sunflowers and tulips for
prices such as had never before been known.   Verrio, a
Neapolitan, covered ceilings and staircases with Gorgons and
Muses, Nymphs and Satyrs, Virtues and Vices, Gods quaffing
5 nectar, and laureled princes riding in triumph.   The income
which he derived from his performances enabled him to keep
one of the most expensive tables in England.   For his pieces
at Windsor alone he received seven thousand pounds, a sum
then sufficient to make a gentleman of moderate wishes per-
10 fectly easy for life, a sum greatly exceeding all that Dryden,
during a literary life of forty years, obtained from the
booksellers.   Verrio's chief assistant and successor, Lewis
Laguerre, came from France.   The two most celebrated
sculptors of that day were also foreigners.   Cibber, whose
15 pathetic emblems of Fury and Melancholy still adorn Bedlam,
was a Dane.   Gibbons, to whose graceful fancy and delicate
touch many of our palaces, colleges, and churches owe their
finest decorations, was a Dutchman.   Even the designs for
the coin were made by French medalists.   Indeed, it was
20 not till the reign of George the Second that our country
could glory in a great painter, and George the Third was on
the throne before she had reason to be proud of any of her
sculptors.

   It is time that this description of the England which
25 Charles the Second governed should draw to a close.   Yet
one subject of the highest moment still remains untouched.
Nothing has as yet been said of the great body of the people,
of those who held the ploughs, who tended the oxen, who
toiled at the looms of Norwich, and squared the Portland
30 stone for Saint Paul's.   Nor can very much be said.   The
most numerous class is precisely the class respecting which
we have the most meagre information.   In those times
philanthropists did not yet regard it as a sacred duty, nor
had demagogues yet found it a lucrative trade, to expatiate

on the distress of the laborer. History was too much occupied with courts and camps to spare a line for the hut of the
peasant or for the garret of the mechanic. The press now
often sends forth in a day a greater quantity of discussion
and declamation about the condition of the working man 5
than was published during the twenty-eight years which
elapsed between the Restoration and the Revolution. But
it would be a great error to infer from the increase of complaint that there has been any increase of misery.

The great criterion of the state of the common people is 10
the amount of their wages; and as four-fifths of the common
people were, in the seventeenth century, employed in agriculture, it is especially important to ascertain what were then
the wages of agricultural industry. On this subject we have
the means of arriving at conclusions sufficiently exact for 15
our purpose.

Sir William Petty, whose mere assertion carries great
weight, informs us that a laborer was by no means in the
lowest state who received for a day's work fourpence with
food or eightpence without food. Four shillings a week, 20
therefore, were, according to Petty's calculation, fair agricultural wages.

That this calculation was not remote from the truth we
have abundant proof. About the beginning of the year 1685,
the justices of Warwickshire, in the exercise of a power 25
intrusted to them by an act of Elizabeth, fixed, at their
quarter sessions, a scale of wages for their county, and notified that every employer who gave more than the authorized
sum and every working man who received more would be
liable to punishment. The wages of the common agricultural 30
laborer, from March to September, they fixed at the precise
sum mentioned by Petty, namely, four shillings a week without food. From September to March the wages were to be
only three and sixpence a week.

But in that age, as in ours, the earnings of the peasant
were very different in different parts of the kingdom.   The
wages of Warwickshire were probably about the average, and
those of the counties near the Scottish border below it.   But
5 there were more favored districts.   In the same year, 1685,
a gentleman of Devonshire, named Richard Dunning, published a small tract, in which he described the condition of
the poor of that county.   That he understood his subject
well it is impossible to doubt; for a few months later his
10 work was reprinted, and was, by the magistrates assembled
in quarter sessions at Exeter, strongly recommended to the
attention of all parochial officers.   According to him, the
wages of the Devonshire peasant were, without food, about
five shillings a week.

15   Still better was the condition of the laborer in the neighborhood of Bury St. Edmund's.   The magistrates of Suffolk
met there in the spring of 1682 to fix a rate of wages, and
resolved that, where the laborer was not boarded, he should
have five shillings a week in winter and six in summer.

20   In 1661 the justices at Chelmsford had fixed the wages
of the Essex laborer, who was not boarded, at six shillings in
winter and seven in summer.   This seems to have been the
highest remuneration given in the kingdom for agricultural
labor between the Restoration and the Revolution; and it
25 is to be observed that, in the year in which this order was
made, the necessaries of life were immoderately dear.   Wheat
was at seventy shillings the quarter, which would even now
be considersd as almost a famine price.

These facts are in perfect accordance with another fact
30 which seems to deserve consideration.   It is evident that, in
a country where no man can be compelled to become a
soldier, the ranks of an army cannot be filled if the government offers much less than the wages of common rustic labor.
At present the pay and beer money of a private in a regiment

of the line amount to seven shillings and sevenpence a week. This stipend, coupled with the hope of a pension, does not attract the English youth in sufficient numbers ; and it is found necessary to supply the deficiency by enlisting largely from among the poorer population of Munster and Connaught. 5 The pay of the private foot soldier in 1685 was only four shillings and eightpence a week; yet it is certain that the government in that year found no difficulty in obtaining many thousands of English recruits at very short notice. The pay of the private foot soldier in the army of the Commonwealth 10 had been seven shillings a week, that is to say, as much as a corporal received under Charles the Second; and seven shillings a week had been found sufficient to fill the ranks with men decidedly superior to the generality of the people. On the whole, therefore, it seems reasonable to conclude that, in 15 the reign of Charles the Second, the ordinary wages of the peasant did not exceed four shillings a week; but that, in some parts of the kingdom, five shillings, six shillings, and, during the summer months, even seven shillings were paid. At present a district where a laboring man earns only seven 20 shillings a week is thought to be in a state shocking to humanity. The average is very much higher; and in prosperous counties, the weekly wages of husbandmen amount to twelve, fourteen, and even sixteen shillings.

The remuneration of workmen employed in manufactures 25 has always been higher than that of the tillers of the soil. In the year 1680 a member of the House of Commons remarked that the high wages paid in this country made it impossible for our textures to maintain a competition with the produce of the Indian looms. An English mechanic, he 30 said, instead of slaving like a native of Bengal for a piece of copper, exacted a shilling a day. Other evidence is extant, which proves that a shilling a day was the pay to which the English manufacturer then thought himself en-

titled, but that he was often forced to work for less.   The
common people of that age were not in the habit of meeting
for public discussion or haranguing or of petitioning parliament.   No newspaper pleaded their cause.   It was in rude
5 rhyme that their love and hatred, their exultation and their
distress found utterance.   A great part of their history is to
be learned only from their ballads.   One of the most remarkable of the popular lays chanted about the streets of Norwich
and Leeds in the time of Charles the Second may still be
10 read on the original broadside.   It is the vehement and
bitter cry of labor against capital.   It describes the good old
times when every artisan employed in the woolen manufacture lived as well as a farmer.   But those times were past.
Sixpence a day now was all that could be earned by hard
15 labor at the loom.   If the poor complained that they could
not live on such a pittance, they were told that they were
free to take it or leave it.   For so miserable a recompense
were the producers of wealth compelled to toil, rising early
and lying down late, while the master clothier, eating, sleep-
20 ing, and idling, became rich by their exertions.   A shilling
a day, the poet declares, is what the weaver would have if
justice were done.*   We may therefore conclude that, in the

* This ballad is in the British Museum.   The precise year is not
given, but the imprimatur of Roger Lestrange fixes the date sufficiently
25 for my purpose.   I will quote some of the lines.   The master clothier
is introduced speaking as follows:

" In former ages we used to give,
So that our workfolks like farmers did live;
But the times are changed, we will make them know.

. . . .

30   We will make them to work hard for sixpence a day,
Though a shilling they deserve if they had their just pay;
If at all they murmur and say, 't is too small,
We bid them choose whether they 'll work at all.

generation which preceded the Revolution, a workman employed in the great staple manufacture of England thought himself fairly paid if he gained six shillings a week.

It may here be noticed that the practice of setting children prematurely to work, a practice which the state, the 5 legitimate protector of those who cannot protect themselves, has, in our time, wisely and humanely interdicted, prevailed in the seventeenth century to an extent which, when compared with the extent of the manufacturing system, seems almost incredible. At Norwich, the chief seat of the cloth- 10 ing trade, a little creature of six years old was thought fit for labor. Several writers of that time, and among them some who were considered as eminently benevolent, mention, with exultation, the fact that in that single city boys and girls of tender age created wealth exceeding what was nec- 15 essary for their own subsistence by twelve thousand pounds a year. The more carefully we examine the history of the past, the more reason shall we find to dissent from those who imagine that our age has been fruitful of new social evils. The truth is that the evils are, with scarcely an 20 exception, old. That which is new is the intelligence which discerns and the humanity which remedies them.

When we pass from the weavers of cloth to a different class of artisans, our inquiries will still lead us to nearly the same conclusions. During several generations, the Commis- 25 sioners of Greenwich Hospital have kept a register of the wages paid to different classes of workmen who have been employed in the repairs of the building. From this valuable

> And thus we do gain all our wealth and estate,
> By many poor men that work early and late. 30
> Then hey for the clothing trade! It goes on brave.
> We scorn for to toyl and moyl, nor yet to slave.
> Our workmen do work hard, but we live at ease,
> We go when we will, and we come when we please."

record it appears that, in the course of a hundred and twenty years, the daily earnings of the bricklayer have risen from half a crown to four and tenpence, those of the mason from half a crown to five and threepence, those of the car-
5 penter from half a crown to five and fivepence, and those of the plumber from three shillings to five and sixpence.

It seems clear, therefore, that the wages of labor, esti-mated in money, were, in 1685, not more than half of what they now are; and there were few articles important to the
10 working man of which the price was not, in 1685, more than half of what it now is. Beer was undoubtedly much cheaper in that age than at present. Meat was also cheaper, but was still so dear that there were hundreds of thousands of families who scarcely knew the taste of it.* In the cost
15 of wheat there has been very little change. The average price of the quarter, during the last twelve years of Charles the Second, was fifty shillings. Bread, therefore, such as is now given to the inmates of a workhouse, was then seldom seen, even on the trencher of a yeoman or of a shopkeeper.
20 The great majority of the nation lived almost entirely on rye, barley, and oats.

The produce of tropical countries, the produce of the mines, the produce of machinery, was positively dearer than at present. Among the commodities for which the laborer
25 would have had to pay higher in 1685 than his posterity pay in 1848 were sugar, salt, coals, candles, soap, shoes, stock-ings, and generally all articles of clothing and all articles of bedding. It may be added that the old coats and blankets would have been, not only more costly, but less serviceable
30 than the modern fabrics.

* King in his *Natural and Political Conclusions* roughly estimated the common people of England at 880,000 families. Of these families 440,000, according to him, ate animal food twice a week. The remain-ing 440,000 ate it not at all, or at most not oftener than once a week.

It must be remembered that those laborers who were able to maintain themselves and their families by means of wages were not the most necessitous members of the community. Beneath them lay a large class which could not subsist without some aid from the parish. There can hardly be a more 5 important test of the condition of the common people than the ratio which this class bears to the whole society. At present the men, women, and children who receive relief are, in bad years, one-tenth of the inhabitants of England and, in good years, one-thirteenth. Gregory King esti- 10 mated them in his time at more than a fifth; and this estimate, which all our respect for his authority will scarcely prevent us from calling extravagant, was pronounced by Davenant eminently judicious.

We are not quite without the means of forming an esti- 15 mate for ourselves. The poor rate was undoubtedly the heaviest tax borne by our ancestors in those days. It was computed, in the reign of Charles the Second, at near seven hundred thousand pounds a year, much more than the produce either of the excise or of the customs, and little less 20 than half the entire revenue of the crown. The poor rate went on increasing rapidly, and appears to have risen in a short time to between eight and nine hundred thousand a year, that is to say, to one-sixth of what it now is. The population was then less than a third of what it now is. The 25 minimum of wages, estimated in money, was half of what it now is; and we can therefore hardly suppose that the average allowance made to a pauper can have been more than half of what it now is. It seems to follow that the proportion of the English people which received parochial relief 30 then must have been larger than the proportion which receives relief now. It is good to speak on such questions with diffidence; but it has certainly never yet been proved that pauperism was a less heavy burden or a less serious

social evil during the last quarter of the seventeenth century
than it has been in our own time.

In one respect it must be admitted that the progress of
civilization has diminished the physical comforts of a por-
5 tion of the poorest class. It has already been mentioned
that, before the Revolution, many thousands of square miles,
now enclosed and cultivated, were marsh, forest, and heath.
Of this wild land much was, by law, common, and much of
what was not common by law was worth so little that the
10 proprietors suffered it to be common in fact. In such a
tract, squatters and trespassers were tolerated to an extent
now unknown. The peasant who dwelt there could, at little
or no charge, procure occasionally some palatable addition
to his hard fare, and provide himself with fuel for the winter.
15 He kept a flock of geese on what is now an orchard rich
with apple blossoms. He snared wild fowl on the fen which
has long since been drained and divided into corn-fields and
turnip-fields. He cut turf among the furze-bushes on the
moor, which is now a meadow bright with clover and re-
20 nowned for butter and cheese. The progress of agriculture
and the increase of population necessarily deprived him of
these privileges. But against this disadvantage a long list
of advantages is to be set off. Of the blessings which civilization and philosophy bring with them a large proportion
25 is common to all ranks, and would, if withdrawn, be missed
as painfully by the laborer as by the peer. The market-
place which the rustic can now reach with his cart in an
hour was, a hundred and sixty years ago, a day's journey
from him. The street which now affords to the artisan,
30 during the whole night, a secure, a convenient, and a bril-
liantly lighted walk was, a hundred and sixty years ago, so
dark after sunset that he would not have been able to see
his hand, so ill paved that he would have run constant risk
of breaking his neck, and so ill watched that he would have

been in imminent danger of being knocked down and plundered of his small earnings. Every bricklayer who falls from a scaffold, every sweeper of a crossing who is run over by a carriage now may have his wounds dressed and his limbs set with a skill such as, a hundred and sixty years ago, all the wealth of a great lord like Ormond or of a merchant prince like Clayton could not have purchased. Some frightful diseases have been extirpated by science, and some have been banishèd by police. The term of human life has been lengthened over the whole kingdom, and especially in the towns. The year 1685 was not accounted sickly; yet in the year 1685 more than one in twenty-three of the inhabitants of the capital died. At present, only one inhabitant of the capital in forty dies annually. The difference in salubrity between the London of the nineteenth century and the London of the seventeenth century is very far greater than the difference between London in an ordinary season and London in the cholera.

Still more important is the benefit which all orders of society, and especially the lower orders, have derived from the mollifying influence of civilization on the national character. The groundwork of that character has indeed been the same through many generations, in the sense in which the groundwork of the character of an individual may be said to be the same when he is a rude and thoughtless schoolboy and when he is a refined and accomplished man. It is pleasing to reflect that the public mind of England has softened while it has ripened, and that we have, in the course of ages, become not only a wiser, but also a kinder people. There is scarcely a page of the history or lighter literature of the seventeenth century which does not contain some proof that our ancestors were less humane than their posterity. The discipline of workshops, of schools, of private families, though not more efficient than at present, was infi-

nitely harsher.   Masters, well born and bred, were in the
habit of beating their servants.   Pedagogues knew no way
of imparting knowledge but by beating their pupils.   Hus-
bands, of decent station, were not ashamed to beat their
5 wives.   The implacability of hostile factions was such as we
can scarcely conceive.   Whigs were disposed to murmur
because Stafford[140] was suffered to die without seeing his
bowels burned before his face.   Tories reviled and insulted
Russell[141] as his coach passed from the Tower to the scaffold
10 in Lincoln's Inn Fields.   As little mercy was shown by the
populace to sufferers of an humbler rank.   If an offender
was put into the pillory, it was well if he escaped with life
from the shower of brickbats and paving stones.   If he was
tied to the cart's tail, the crowd pressed round him, implor-
15 ing the hangman to give it to the fellow well, and make him
howl.   Gentlemen arranged parties of pleasure to Bridewell
on court days, for the purpose of seeing the wretched women
who beat hemp there whipped.   A man pressed to death
for refusing to plead, a woman burned for coining excited
20 less sympathy than is now felt for a galled horse or an over-
driven ox.   Fights, compared with which a boxing match is
a refined and humane spectacle, were among the favorite
diversions of a large part of the town.   Multitudes assembled to see gladiators hack each other to pieces with
25 deadly weapons, and shouted with delight when one of the
combatants lost a finger or an eye.   The prisons were hells
on earth, seminaries of every crime and of every disease.
At the assizes the lean and yellow culprits brought with
them from their cells to the dock an atmosphere of stench
30 and pestilence which sometimes avenged them signally on
bench, bar, and jury.   But on all this misery society looked
with profound indifference.[142]   Nowhere could be found that
sensitive and restless compassion which has, in our time, extended a powerful protection to the factory child, to the

Hindoo widow, to the negro slave, which pries into the stores and water-casks of every emigrant ship, which winces at every lash laid on the back of a drunken soldier, which will not suffer the thief in the hulks to be ill fed or overworked, and which has repeatedly endeavored to save the life even 5 of the murderer. It is true that compassion ought, like all other feelings, to be under the government of reason, and has, for want of such government, produced some ridiculous and some deplorable effects. But the more we study the annals of the past, the more shall we rejoice that we live in 10 a merciful age, in an age in which cruelty is abhorred, and in which pain, even when deserved, is inflicted reluctantly and from a sense of duty. Every class doubtless has gained largely by this great moral change; but the class which has gained most is the poorest, the most dependent, and the 15 most defenceless. .

The general effect of the evidence which has been submitted to the reader seems hardly to admit of doubt. Yet, in spite of evidence, many will still image to themselves the England of the Stuarts as a more pleasant country than the 20 England in which we live. It may at first sight seem strange that society, while constantly moving forward with eager speed, should be constantly looking backward with tender regret. But these two propensities, inconsistent as they may appear, can easily be resolved into the same principle. Both 25 spring from our impatience of the state in which we actually are. That impatience, while it stimulates us to surpass preceding generations, disposes us to overrate their happiness. It is, in some sense, unreasonable and ungrateful in us to be constantly discontented with a condition which is constantly 30 improving. But, in truth, there is constant improvement precisely because there is constant discontent. If we were perfectly satisfied with the present, we should cease to contrive, to labor, and to save with a view to the future. And it is natural that, being dissatisfied with the present, we should form a too favorable estimate of the past.

In truth we are under a deception similar to that which misleads the traveler in the Arabian desert.   Beneath the
5 caravan all is dry and bare; but far in advance and far in the rear is the semblance of refreshing waters.   The pilgrims hasten forward and find nothing but sand where, an hour before, they had seen a lake.   They turn their eyes and see a lake where, an hour before, they were toiling through
10 sand.   A similar illusion seems to haunt nations through every stage of the long progress from poverty and barbarism to the highest degrees of opulence and civilization.   But if we resolutely chase the mirage backward, we shall find it recede before us into the regions of fabulous antiquity.   It
15 is now the fashion to place the golden age of England in times when noblemen were destitute of comforts the want of which would be intolerable to a modern footman, when farmers and shopkeepers breakfasted on loaves the very sight of which would raise a riot in a modern workhouse,
20 when men died faster in the purest country air than they now die in the most pestilential lanes of our towns, and when men died faster in the lanes of our towns than they now die on the coast of Guiana.   We too shall, in our turn, be out-stripped, and in our turn be envied.   It may well be, in the
25 twentieth century, that the peasant of Dorsetshire may think himself miserably paid with fifteen shillings a week; that the carpenter at Greenwich may receive ten shillings a day; that laboring men may be as little used to dine without meat as they now are to eat rye bread; that sanitary police and medi-
30 cal discoveries may have added several more years to the average length of human life; that numerous comforts and luxuries which are now unknown, or confined to a few, may be within the reach of every diligent and thrifty working **man.   And yet it may then be the mode to assert that the**

increase of wealth and the progress of science have benefited the few at the expense of the many, and to talk of the reign of Queen Victoria as the time when England was truly merry England, when all classes were bound together by brotherly sympathy, when the rich did not grind the faces of the poor, 5 and when the poor did not envy the splendor of the rich.

NOTES.

This account, which is the third chapter of Macaulay's "History of England," is a general statement of the condition of the country, not only in the year 1685, but during the reign of Charles II. It is of especial interest when contrasted with the present century on the one hand or with the time of Elizabeth on the other. A book like Huxley's "Advance of Science" gives a view of England in the middle of this century, while Froude's "English Seamen" shows much of the condition of the kingdom in the sixteenth.

1. Charles II returned to England and took possession of the throne that had been his father's, in 1660. This is called the Restoration. He died in 1685, and was succeeded by his brother under the title of James II.

2. The Plantagenets were Henry II, 1154–1189; Richard I, 1189–1199; John, 1199–1216; Henry III, 1216–1272; Edward I, 1272–1307; Edward II, 1307–1327; Edward III, 1327–1377; Richard II, 1377–1399. The Tudors were Henry VII, 1485–1509; Henry VIII, 1509–1547; Edward VI, 1547–1553; Mary (called Bloody), 1553–1559; Elizabeth, 1559–1603. The Stuarts were James I, 1603–1625; Charles I, 1625–1649; Charles II, 1660–1685; James II, 1685–1701.* The passage amounts to the statement that the wealth of England was greater in the fifteenth and sixteenth centuries than from the twelfth to the fourteenth; greater in the seventeenth than in the sixteenth.

3. The Long Parliament assembled in 1640, and continued through the remaining years of Charles I, through the Commonwealth and Protectorate, being dissolved only in the year of the Restoration, 1660.

4. The Great Plague devastated London in 1665. A hundred thousand persons are said to have died of it in six months. In 1666 the Great Fire burned September 2–6, destroying eighty-nine churches, including St. Paul's Cathedral, and more than thirteen hundred dwellings, — two-thirds of the entire city in all.

5. A clerk whose duty it is to record the acts of a legislative body.

* Throughout these notes the dates in the case of sovereigns are those of the beginning and end of reign.

6. Written in 1848.

7. Moss-troopers, a term applied to the maurauders who lived neaɪ the borders of England and Scotland, plundering across the line. The name comes from the mosses or bogs through which they made their way by paths known only to themselves.

8. George III. 1760–1820.

9. "The Duke [of Northumberland] tells me his people in Keeldar were all quite wild the first time his father went up to shoot there. The women had no other dress than a bed-gown and petticoat. The men were savage and could hardly be brought to rise from the heath, either from sullenness or fear. They sang a wild tune, the burden of which was *Ourina, ourina, ourina.* The females sang, the men danced round, and at a certain part of the tune they drew their dirks, which they always wore." — Sir Walter Scott, "Journal," October 7, 1827.

10. Hearth-money, or chimney-money, was a tax of a crown for each chimney in a house.

11. The Cabal (1667–1673) was the name given to a ministry formed in the reign of Charles II. The word means a secret committee, and, rather curiously, the initials of the members of this ministry formed the word: Clifford, Arlington, Buckingham, Ashley-Cooper (Lord Shaftesbury), and Lauderdale. They agreed in wishing to strengthen the power of the king. Cabal has since their time, in the words of Macaulay, "never been used except as a term of reproach."

12. Thomas Osborne, afterward Duke of Leeds, was successively Treasurer, Privy Councillor, and Lord High Treasurer under Charles II, being at the time Earl of Danby. He was afterwards Prime Minister under William. He was twice impeached for corruption, but managed to escape conviction, although it was proved that he had received a bribe of 5500 guineas from the East India Company. He died in 1712.

13. The Revolution. The expulsion of James II, and the seating of William and Mary on the throne in 1688–1689.

14. Henry IV of France, founder of the Bourbon dynasty, 1589–1610. Philip II of Spain, 1556–1598, husband of Mary, Queen of England.

15. Parma, Duke of, Alessandro Farnese, general of Philip II in the Netherlands. Died, 1592.

16. Spinola, Spanish general. Died, 1630.

17. Richelieu, Cardinal de, Prime Minister of Louis XIII of France. Died, 1642.

18. Fairfax, Lord Thomas, English Parliamentary general under Cromwell. Died, 1671. Cromwell, Oliver, Puritan general, at the head of the government from the defeat of Charles I, and Lord Protector, 1653–1658.

19. Vauban, French military engineer. Died, 1707.

20. Louis XIV of France, called the Great, 1643–1715.

21. The name Cavaliers was given to the party of Charles I, as distinguished from the Roundheads, or Puritans. In the civil war which resulted in the execution of Charles I, the soldiers of Cromwell committed many excesses upon the possessions of the Royalists and upon the established churches.

22. Fifth Monarchy men were an extreme sect of the period of the Puritan Revolution, largely found in Cromwell's army, and believing that his government was the beginning of the "Fifth Monarchy," in which Christ was to return to the earth. The other four monarchies were the Assyrian, Persian, Grecian, and Roman.

23. Maurice of Nassau, Prince of Orange, son of William the Silent, Dutch general. Died, 1625.

24. Ossory, Lord, Irish general.

25. Naseby, battle of. One of the decisive engagements in the struggle of Charles I against Parliament. It was fought on July 14, 1645, and resulted in the complete victory of the Parliamentary troops under Fairfax and Cromwell.

26. Five years later, September 3, 1650, the Parliamentarians under Cromwell, Monk, and Lambert defeated the Scots, the champions of Charles II, at Dunbar. It was on this occasion, when the sun scattered the mist and showed the rout of the enemy, that Cromwell uttered his famous quotation: "Let God arise and let His enemies be scattered."

27. The Spanish Armada was the mighty fleet sent out by Philip II of Spain against England in 1588. Broken by the English fleet in the Channel, it was afterwards scattered by storm and completely destroyed. An excellent account of the whole matter will be found in Froude's "English Seamen in the Sixteenth Century."

28. Blake, Robert, English admiral, 1597–1657.

29. Pepys, Samuel, Secretary of the English Navy under Charles II. He left a diary in shorthand, which has since been deciphered, and which is one of the most famous works of its kind in existence. It gives a very vivid and intimate picture of the court of Charles II.

30. Cimon was an Athenian commander, son of Miltiades. Died, 449 B.C. Lysander, a Spartan commander, killed, 395 B.C. Pompey, a Roman general, triumvir with Cæsar and Crassus, murdered in Egypt, 48 B.C. Agrippa, Roman commander, died, 12 B.C.

31. Flodden Field, 1513. James IV of Scotland overwhelmed by the English.

32. Jarnac, a town in western France, where in 1569 the Huguenots, the French Protestants, were defeated by the troops of Charles IX, commanded by his brother, afterward Henry III. Moncontour, another battle where the Huguenots were again defeated in the same year.

33. Louis, Prince of Condé.

34. John of Austria, Don, Spanish commander, half-brother of Philip II. Died, 1578.

35. Charles Howard, English admiral. Died, 1624.

36. Sir Walter Raleigh, favorite of Queen Elizabeth, navigator, discoverer, and author. His greatest work was a "History of the World," written in the Tower, and left unfinished. Beheaded under James I, 1618.

37. Two generals in the Parliamentary army in the struggle against Charles I.

38. Formerly the Thames was much used as a thoroughfare, and the palace of Whitehall had a boat-landing on the river.

39. Hampton Court, a palace originally built by Cardinal Wolsey, is a dozen miles southwest of London. It was by him presented to Henry VIII. It has since been occupied by Cromwell, the Stuarts, William III, and the first two Georges. It contains a fine collection of pictures, and is much visited.

40. Sir John Narborough, English naval officer and discoverer. He suppressed the pirates of Tripoli in 1675. Died, 1688 Sir Cloudesley Shovel, English admiral. Drowned, 1707.

41. Smollett, Tobias George, English novelist and historian, 1721–1771. His best-known novels are "The Adventures of Roderick Random," "The Adventures of Peregrine Pickle," and "The Expedition of Humphry Clinker." His novels are full of vigor and movement, but are very coarse.

42. "Poundage . . . an allowance or abatement of twelve Pence in the Pound, upon the receipt of a Summ of Money." — E. Phillips, 1706.

43. The groom of the stole is the first lord of the bedchamber in the English royal household.

44. Salisbury Plain, an immense rolling down near the city of Salisbury. In the midst of it stands the famous ancient ruin called Stonehenge.

45. John Evelyn, in his Diary, writes, June 2, 1676: "I went with my Lord Chamberlaine to see a garden in Enfield town; thence to see Mr. Sec. Coventry's lodge in the Chace. It is a very pretty place, the house commodious, the gardens handsome, and our entertainment very free, there being none but my Lord and myself. That which I most wondered at was that in the compass of 25 miles, yet within 14 of London, there is not a house, barn, church, or building, beside three lodges. To this lodge are three great ponds and some few enclousures, the rest a solitary desert, yet stored with not less than 3000 deer."

46. Queen Anne, the daughter of James II, reigned from 1702 until 1714.

47. As George II came to the throne in 1727, the time to the writing of this history would be practically about a hundred and twenty years.

48. A book in which were entered the expenses of the household of the Duke of Northumberland in the fifteenth century.

49. The Rock of Gibraltar and the two hills of the African side of the strait, so called from the old belief that Hercules set them up to mark the western limit of his travels when he went for the apples of Hesperides.

50. Two of the mistresses of Charles II. To both of them he gave large sums. Nell Gwynn was a popular actress, and the last words of the king were: "Don't let poor Nelly starve."

51. Glastonbury Abbey is said to be the only religious foundation in England which has kept its existence from Roman times. It was traditionally said to be the burial place of King Arthur and of St. Patrick, as well as undoubtedly containing the tomb of St. Dunstan. It was up to the Reformation a see of great wealth and importance. Its last abbot was by order of Henry VIII hanged.

52. Reading, the chief town in Berkshire, comes into history with a battle in 871, in which Ethelred, the father of Alfred, was defeated. Henry I founded here a great monastery in which he was afterward buried. The see was, like Glastonbury, of great importance, wealth, and influence, until the monasteries were overthrown under Henry VIII.

53. William of Wykeham was Bishop of Winchester and Chancellor under Edward III. He was driven from court on false charges, but afterward restored to honor. He retired in 1391 to private life, and founded New College, Oxford. He was a man so blameless of life that a contemporary said of him that to attempt to find a fault in him was like endeavoring to find a knot in a rush. Died, 1404.

54. William of Waynflete was also Bishop of Winchester and Chancellor; but in the fifteenth century. He founded Magdalen College, Oxford. He was the warm friend of Henry VI. Died, 1486.

55. The high intellectual and moral worth of the men by whom Queen Elizabeth was surrounded was by no means the least brilliant feature of her time. William Cecil, Lord Burleigh, was Secretary of State under Edward IV, and reassumed the office almost immediately when Elizabeth succeeded Mary. For forty years he enjoyed the confidence of the astute Elizabeth, and richly deserved it. He died in 1598. Sir Nicholas Bacon, the father of Sir Francis, was Elizabeth's Lord-Keeper of the Great Seal. His son described him as "a plain man, direct and constant, without all finesse and doubleness." He died 1579. Roger Ascham was tutor to

Elizabeth, and an author of learning and distinction. He was one of the earliest English Greek scholars. His best-known books are " The Schole-master" and " Toxophilus," the latter a treatise on archery. Died, 1568. Sir Thomas Smith was a zealous friend of the Reformation, was Secretary of State under Edward VI, and an associate of Lord Burleigh under Eliza-beth. He was sent upon important missions. Died, 1577. Sir Walter Mildmay, Chancellor of the Exchequer and founder of Emanuel College, Cambridge. Died, 1589. Sir Francis Walsingham, called " the most pene-trating statesman of his time," was of sagacity and insight so great that in the next century it was said : " He saw every man and none saw him." With every opportunity of amassing wealth by corrupt means he died so poor as hardly to leave enough for his burial. He was one of the instru-ments in the conviction of Mary, Queen of Scots, of treason. Died, 1590.

56. Matthew Parker, Archbishop of Canterbury, died 1575. Edmund Grindal, Archbishop of Canterbury, died 1583. After the Reformation the revenues of the English prelates were greatly reduced, and under Elizabeth and her successors the prelates had no opportunity of amassing large for-tunes, such as those possessed by their predecessors under Catholic rule.

57. Thomas Wolsey, Archbishop of York, was the son of a butcher, who by his ability and sagacity rose to the highest influence and wealth under Henry VIII. He was made cardinal and legate by Pope Leo X, and prime minister by the king. He enjoyed the revenues of several sees, gathered an enormous fortune, and lived in a splendor more than regal. His fall was occasioned by his want of zeal in serving Henry in procuring the divorce from Catherine of Arragon, and he died in disgrace in 1530, on his way to London to be tried for high treason. His words in his last hours have become famous, although in the version of Shakespeare rather than his own : " Had I but served God as diligently as I have served the King, He would not have given me over in my gray hairs."

> " Had I but served my God with half the zeal
> I served my king, He would not in mine age
> Have left me naked to mine enemies."
> *Henry VIII,* iii, 2.

58. William Laud, Archbishop of Canterbury under Charles I. A man of purity of life, but of great intolerance and severity. He was charged with treason by the Parliamentarian party after the death of Charles, and although the charges could not be satisfactorily established, he was exe-cuted in 1645.

59. Clarendon, Earl of, minister of Charles I, Lord Chancellor under Charles II, author of several histories. He died in exile in France in 1674.

60. Jonathan Swift, Dean of St. Patrick's, Dublin, 1667–1745. One of the most brilliant and caustic writers of the eighteenth century. His most famous works are " The Tale of a Tub " and " Gulliver's Travels." The passage alluded to is from a satirical essay called " Directions for Servants."

61. Hobbes, English philosophical writer, known chiefly by a work called " Leviathan, or the Matter, Form, and Power of a Commonwealth, Ecclesiastical and Civil," published in 1651. Died, 1679. Bossuet was a learned French bishop and author. Died, 1704.

62. George Villiers, Duke of Buckingham, was one of the most brilliant and corrupt nobles of the dissolute court of Charles II. Dryden has given a description of him, under the name Zimri, in the famous political satire, " Absalom and Achitophel ":

> ' A man so various that he seem'd to be
> Not one but all mankind's epitome;
> Stiff in opinions, always in the wrong,
> Was everything by starts, and nothing long;
> But, in the course of one revolving moon,
> Was chemist, fiddler, statesman, and buffoon.
> Then all for women, painting, rhyming, drinking,
> Besides ten thousand freaks that died in thinking.
> Blest madman! who could every hour employ
> With something new to wish or to enjoy.
> Railing and praising were his usual themes,
> And both, to show his judgments, in extremes.
> So over-violent or over-civil,
> That every man with him was God or devil.
> In squandering wealth was his peculiar art,
> Nothing went unrewarded but desert;
> Beggar'd by fools whom still he found too late;
> He had his jest, and they had his estate.
> He laugh'd himself from court, then had relief
> By forming parties, but could ne'er be chief."

He died in 1688. " The truest type of the time," writes Green, " is the Duke of Buckingham, and the most characteristic event in the Duke's life was a duel in which he consummated his seduction of Lady Shrewsbury by killing her husband, while the Countess in disguise as a page held his horse for him, and looked on at the murder."

63. George Saville, Marquis of Halifax, Lord Privy Seal under James II, and afterward under William and Mary. Died, 1695. He published a tract called the " Character of a Trimmer," in which he defended his position as an independent, belonging to neither party, but as " trimming " from one side to the other as the public interest required.

64. " Lawn sleeves " is a phrase not infrequently used to designate a bishop, these being a conspicuous portion of the dress. The scarlet hood, worn hanging down the back, is the badge of certain high university degrees.

65. The Conventicle Act of 1664 imposed a fine on any person over sixteen years of age for being present at any assembly — or "conventicle " — for holding worship otherwise than according to the Church of England. The Five Mile Act of the following year forbade nonconformist clergymen to come within five miles of any corporate town or place where they had once ministered. Both acts belonged to what was known as the "Clarendon Code," a series of measures for the suppression of "dissenters," or "nonconformists," those who refused to conform to the forms of worship of the Church of England.

66. The Exclusionists were supporters of the bill first passed by the Commons in 1679, disabling the Duke of York, afterwards James II, as a Papist, from succeeding Charles II. The bill was passed by the Commons in three successive parliaments, but in each case the parliament was dissolved by Charles, so that the bill never became a law.

67. The crime of crimping or kidnapping youths for slavery in America or in the East Indies continued in England well on in the eighteenth century. Stevenson's novel, "Kidnapped," takes its name from an attempt thus to get rid of the hero.

68. Eli Whitney, a Massachusetts man, inventor of the cotton gin. Died, 1825. Sir Richard Arkwright, inventor of the spinning frame, or "spinning jenny." Died, 1792.

69. Whittle is an old term for knife. The word is used once by Shakespeare, and still exists in some of the rural dialects of England.

70. Geoffrey Chaucer, born about 1340, and died 1400, is called the "father of English poetry." He is the first English author of permanent importance. His most famous work, " The Canterbury Tales," still remains one of the great classics of the language.

71. Dr. Samuel Johnson, 1709–1784, was one of the most famous of English men of letters in the middle of the eighteenth century. He is best remembered as the author of the first general dictionary of the English tongue and as the subject of Boswell's " Life of Johnson," the most remarkable biography in the language.

72. James II, the second son of Charles I, was in his infancy created Duke of York. All the income from the postal service was settled upon him in the reign of his brother, Charles II. See later in the chapter.

73. Tunbridge Wells, thirty-one miles southeast of London, where chalybeate springs were discovered in 1606, was one of the most fashionable watering-places of the eighteenth century.

74. Basset was a game of cards resembling faro, enormously popular among the fashionable gamblers of London after the Restoration.

75. The name morris was probably originally Moresco, or some word indicating that the dance was derived from the Moors. It was performed by players whose costume was hung with small bells, and was a conspicuous part of English Christmas sports as early as the fourteenth century.

76. Bramante d'Urbino, 1444–1514, a celebrated Italian architect, who began the present church of St. Peter's at Rome. Palladio was also an Italian architect, but of reputation inferior to that of Bramante; 1518–1580.

77. Christopher Anstey was a satirical poet, of more reputation in his own day than since. He lived in the latter part of the eighteenth century, dying in 1805, and made a great success by "The New Bath Guide." For Smollett, see note 41. Frances Burney, best known by her novel "Evelina," died at Bath, 1840, at the age of eighty-eight. By marriage she was Madame d'Arblay. Jane Austen, 1775–1817, still holds rank as one of the finest women novelists of the language. Her best-known books are "Sense and Sensibility," "Pride and Prejudice," "Emma," and "Persuasion." All these writers describe life and society at Bath as it was in the last century, when that city was a fashionable resort and watering-place.

78. John Hampden, 1594–1643, and John Pym, 1584–1643, headed the attacks of the Commons upon the government of Charles I.

79. Richard Cromwell, the son of Oliver, 1626–1712, succeeded his father as Lord Protector in 1658. He was, however, forced to resign in the following year.

80. The Earl of Shaftesbury, 1621–1683, was at first on the side of Charles I, in his struggle with the Commons; then joined with the latter; quarreled with Cromwell, and was excluded from parliament. He was one of the deputation sent to invite Charles II to return to England, and under this monarch he became Lord Chancellor. He was involved in numerous intrigues, and was at last forced to flee to Holland, where he died. He figures in "Absalom and Achitophel" as the latter personage, being described as

> "For close designs and crooked counsels fit,
> Sagacious, bold, and turbulent of wit;
> Restless, unfixed in principles and place,
> In power displeased, impatient of disgrace.
> A fiery soul, which, working out its way,
> Fretted the pigmy body to decay,
> And o'er-informed the tenement of clay.
> A daring pilot in extremity;
> Pleased with the danger when the waves went high,
> He fought the storms; but, for a calm unfit,

> Would steer too near the sands to show his wit. . . .
> Yet fame deserved no enemy can grudge;
> The statesman we abhor, but praise the judge.
> In Israel's courts ne'er sat an Abethdin
> With more discerning eyes, or hands more clean;
> Unbrib'd, unsought, the wretched to redress;
> Swift of dispatch, and easy of access."

81. Inigo Jones, 1572–1652, was the most famous architect of his time.

82. Somers, John, Lord, 1652–1716, one of the most able statesmen of the epoch of the Revolution.

83. John Tillotson, 1630–1694, famous English divine and Archbishop of Canterbury.

84. John Dryden, 1631–1700, poet, playwright, satirist, and essayist. His most famous works are "Absalom and Achitophel," "Ode on St. Cecilia's Day" (first and second), and "The Hind and the Panther." For the honor in which he was held in his old age, see later in the account of the coffee-houses.

85. Sir Isaac Newton, 1642–1727, conceived the theory of gravitation about 1666, and presented to the Royal Society in 1686 his famous " Principia," which set forth the theory as applied to the system of the universe. The "Principia" was published in the following year.

86. Sir Robert Walpole, Earl of Orford, 1676–1745, Prime Minister under George I. He maintained his power by the most wholesale bribery and corruption, but he preserved peace at a time when it was essential to the prosperity of England. William Pitt, Earl of Chatham, 1708–1778, called "the great commoner," was Prime Minister under both George II and George III. He warmly advocated conciliatory measures in the treatment of the American colonies, although opposed to their complete freedom.

87. The battle of Worcester was fought September 3, 1651, during the unsuccessful attempt of Charles II to obtain the throne left vacant by the execution of his father. The Scotch Royalist forces were beaten by Cromwell, and Charles put to flight, this engagement closing the campaign.

88. Andrew Marvel was a Parliamentary poet and satirist, famous for his attacks on the government of Charles II. Three of his poems are given in the "Golden Treasury," numbered lxv, cxl, and cxiv. The first, the "Horatian Ode" to Cromwell, is one of his best-known lyrics.

89. John Sobieski was king of Poland, 1674–1696. Doge was the title of the chief magistrate of Venice and of Genoa, the office being elective, at first for life, but afterward for a fixed term. The office continued in Venice from the eighth, and in Genoa from the fourteenth, to the end of the eighteenth century. Lawrence Hyde, Earl of Rochester, son of the great

Earl of Clarendon, became First Lord of the Treasury in 1679. He was opposed to Lord Halifax in the struggle to exclude the Duke of York, afterward James II, from the succession on account of his religion. He died in 1711. His dissolute character is sufficiently indicated elsewhere in the chapter.

90. The Duke of Monmouth was a natural son of Charles II, born while that prince was in exile, 1649. As Charles had no legitimate heir, a design was formed to secure the succession for Monmouth. Charles refused to countenance the idea, and twice banished his son to Holland. After the death of Charles, Monmouth raised troops, and had himself proclaimed king ; but his forces were routed by those of James II in the battle of Sedgemoor, and he was soon after captured and executed.

91. The foolish trick of affected pronunciation has been the badge of the fop for centuries. The Roman satirists made merry over it; Ben Jonson jeered at the dandies who in the days of Elizabeth affected an Italian accent. In our own day there is plenty of jesting over the affectations of those who imitate English speech. At the time of which Macaulay writes the fashionable dialect was chiefly notable by the pronunciation of *o* like *a*. Lord Foppingham is a character in the comedy of Sir John Vanbrugh, 1666–1726, called "The Relapse." Foppingham is a wealthy fool who has just purchased a title, and the manner in which he is represented as talking is probably a fair, if somewhat extreme, example of the manner of the time:

"Amanda. The inside of a book should recommend it most to us.

"Lord Fop. That, I must confess, I am not altogether so fand of. Far to my mind the inside of a book is to entertain one's self with the forced product of another man's brain. Naw I think a man of quality and breeding may be much diverted with the natural sprauts of his own," etc.

92. Charles Perrault, 1628–1703, a French writer who espoused warmly the cause of modern literature as opposed to classical. The quarrel between Perrault and Boileau concerning the relative merits of the ancients and moderns lasted a dozen years. He is remembered to-day by his collection of fairy tales, " *Les contes de ma mère l'oye*," "Tales of my Mother Goose."

93. Nicholas Boileau-Despréaux, 1636–1711, a famous French critic and poet. He was the father of French criticism, and his "*Art poétique*" is the book upon which were based the theories of the school of poetry in England of which Pope was the head.

94. "Venice Preserved," a tragedy by Thomas Otway, 1651–1685, was very popular in its time. It is hardly necessary to remark upon Milton's "Paradise Lost," mentioned in the previous line, except to note that in the latter part of the seventeenth century the question whether epic and dramatic poetry should be in blank verse or rhyme was very earnestly debated. Dryden at first wrote tragedies in rhyme, and vigorously defended the practice ; but he afterward changed his views.

95. Jean Baptiste Racine, 1639–1699, was one of the most celebrated of French dramatic poets. Some of his plays yet keep the French stage, and one, at least, the " Phèdre," has been in late years played in this country by Sara Bernhardt and Madame Duse. René Le Bossu, a French abbé, published in 1675 a " Traité du poëme épique," a work of more note then than it has been since.

96. The adventure at Gadshill is told by Shakespeare in the second act of the First Part of King Henry IV. Gadshill in more recent times became the home of Charles Dickens.

97. Boniface is a rascally landlord in Farquhar's comedy, " Beaux' Stratagem." He furnished information of the movements of travelers to Gibbet, the highwayman. The name has come to be used as a general term for an innkeeper.

97a. The allusion is of course to Chaucer, who in the prologue to the " Canterbury Tales " makes the personages who were going on the pilgrimage gather at the Tabard Inn.

> " Bifil that in that seson on a day
> In Southwerk at the Tabbard as I lay,
> Redy to wenden on my pilgrimage
> To Caunterbury with full devout corage,
> At nyght were come into that hostelyre
> Wel nyne and twenty in a compaignye
> Of sondry folk."

98. William Shenstone, English poet, 1714–1763. His best-known work is the " Schoolmistress," one of the earliest examples of modern realism. The reference in the text is to an often-quoted verse, said to have been written by Shenstone on the window of an inn :

> " Whoe'er has travelled life's dull round,
> Where'er his stages may have been,
> May sigh to think he still has found
> The warmest welcome of an inn."

99. Sir Edmundbury Godfrey was the London magistrate before whom Titus Oates made a deposition concerning the so-called Popish Plot in 1681. Godfrey was soon afterward found in a ditch dead from a sword-thrust. It was at once assumed that he had been murdered by the Catholics, and immense excitement resulted. Edward Coleman was secretary to the Duchess of York. He was accused by Oates, and among his papers, seized when he was arrested, were found letters to the confessor of Louis XIV asking for money to be employed in giving "the greatest blow to the Protestant religion it has received since its birth."

100. Titus Oates was a worthless and unscrupulous adventurer, a clergy-man convicted of perjury, who devised the story of the so-called Popish Plot. He alleged that a general massacre of Protestants by the Catholics was intended. The assassination of Godfrey and the papers of Coleman gave so strong a color of probability to the tale that it was generally received as true by the Protestants. The agitation was fostered by Shaftes-bury for political purposes, and when he had gained his ends it died out for want of fuel. Oates was pilloried and sentenced to imprisonment. He was, however, released after the Revolution.

101. The Janizaries were the body-guard of the sultan of Turkey. The troop was organized in the fourteenth century, and became so large and powerful as practically to restrict greatly the power of the sultan. In 1826 the Janizaries were destroyed by a revolt contrived by Mahmud II, and by the massacre by which it was followed.

102. Blaise Pascal, 1623–1662, was a celebrated French mathematician, philosopher, and author. Jean Baptiste Poquelin Molière, 1622–1673, was the greatest French writer of comedies and one of the most brilliant geniuses of all literature, except for the four or five of the world's greatest.

103. Dante Alighieri, 1265–1321, the greatest of Italian poets, author of the "Vita Nuova" and the "Divine Comedy." It is usual to regard Shakespeare, Homer, and Dante as the greatest writers of all time. Tor-quato Tasso, 1544–1595, a celebrated Italian poet. His most famous poem is "Jerusalem Delivered."

104. Johann Wolfgang von Goethe, 1749–1832, was the chief poet and one of the great novelists of Germany. His most famous poem is "Faust"; his most celebrated novel "Wilhelm Meister." Friedrich von Schiller, 1759–1805, a famous German poet, the friend of Goethe. He produced numerous plays and works in prose and in verse. His poetic plays, "Wallenstein," "Maria Stuart," and "William Tell" are best known.

105. Lady Jane Grey, 1537–1554, the beautiful and ill-fated instrument of the ambition of the Duke of Northumberland, who for eleven days after the death of Edward VI bore the title of queen. The throne being then taken by Mary, Lady Jane was imprisoned in the Tower and afterward beheaded. Lucy Hutchinson, 1620–1659, was the daughter of Sir John Apsley and wife of Colonel John Hutchinson. After the death of her husband she wrote his memoirs, and this book is so valuable from the light that it throws on the period covered by it as to be still an authority. As both Lady Jane Grey and Mrs. Hutchinson were notable for the high

cultivation of their minds, Macaulay uses them as a type contrasting sharply with the unintellectual women of whom he is writing.

106. After the Restoration there came into fashion a certain sort of enormously long and enormously sentimental romance then in vogue in France. Two of the most popular of these stories were the " Clelia " and " The Grand Cyrus."

107. Philaris was a tyrant of Agrigentum in Sicily, in the sixth century B.C. He is said to have roasted his enemies in a brazen bull so contrived that the cries of the victims were made to sound like the natural bellowing of that animal. Certain epistles which it was claimed were written by him were discovered or forged in the sixteenth century, and much discussion as to their genuineness ensued. Richard Bentley, 1662–1742, is held to have proved them to be fictitious.

108. Lucius Cary, Viscount Falkland, killed in the battle of Newbury, 1643, fighting on the side of the Royalists. He was a politician and man of letters, one of the comparatively limited number of classical scholars in England in his time.

109. Charles James Fox, son of Lord Holland, 1749–1806, an English statesman and orator. He supported the cause of the American colonies during the Revolution, and took a conspicuous part in the impeachment of Warren Hastings. William Windham, 1750–1810, English statesman and orator. George Grenville, 1712–1770, statesman, Prime Minister under George III. For Pitt, see note 86. The passage emphasizes the intellectual inefficiency of the seventeenth century by contrasting its scholarship with that of the statesmen in the preceding and following centuries.

110. Augustus, Caius Julius Cæsar Octavianus, or more briefly Augustus Cæsar, was the first Roman Emperor. He was born 63 B.C., and became undisputed master of the empire in 31 B.C., although not receiving the title " Augustus " until 27 B.C. He died 14 A.D. In his reign Roman literature reached its highest development. So great was the time of his reign that the term " Augustan Age " became typical of peace and prosperity. He gave his name to the month August, and Jesus Christ was born during his reign. Virgil, Horace, and Ovid, the Latin poets, were all patronized by Augustus, and all wrote in his praise.

111. This account of the way in which the French language became chief among continental tongues, and in England replaced both Latin and Greek and the Italian which was the fashionable language at the time of Elizabeth is the more interesting from the fact that up to the present time French has continued the means of communication between persons of different tongues. English is, however, now largely recognized as coming into somewhat the same use.

112. Jean de la Fontaine, 1621–1695, a French author chiefly celebrated for his twelve books of fables in verse. For Bossuet, see note 61 ; Racine, note 95; and Molière, note 102.

113. John Donne, 1573–1631, English poet and divine.

114. Abraham Cowley, 1618–1667, English poet. He is represented in the " Golden Treasury " by the poem numbered cii.

115. The Puritan custom of giving to their children whole scriptural phrases as names is well known. A striking example is Praisegod Barebones, a member of Cromwell's Parliament. He is said to have had two brothers, one named Christ-came-into-the-world-to-save, and the other If-Christ-had-not-died-thou-hadst-been-damned. That human nature is much the same in all ages is illustrated by the fact that the irreverent are said to have abbreviated the latter name into its last syllable. The horror of the Puritans at all festive celebrations was intensified when they saw in a feast anything relating to the Roman Catholic faith ; and thus they especially condemned plum-puddings and mince pies as connected with the Church observance of Christmas. Jack in the Green was a character in the May Day sports, represented by a lad decorated with flowers and standing amid rings or hoops of evergreen.

116. Richard Crashaw, 1616–1650, English poet. A charming specimen of his verse is given in the " Golden Treasury," lxxix.

117. There were a number of remarkable sects developed among the Puritans. The Supralapsarians held the doctrine that before the fall of man God had already destined some to eternal life and others to eternal death.

118. Edmund Waller, 1605–1687, English poet. His best-known and most delicate poem is " Go, Lovely Rose," " Golden Treasury," lxxxix.

118a. The allusion is of course to John Milton, 1608–1674, and to his great epic, " Paradise Lost," published in 1667.

119. Samuel Butler, 1612–1680, is remembered by the very clever and very bitter satire on Puritanism, " Hudibras." The poem was a great favorite with Charles II.

120. Ben Jonson, 1573(?)–1637, a celebrated dramatist and poet of the Elizabethan period. His most important plays are " Volpone," " Epicœne, or the Silent Woman," " Every Man in His Humor," and the " Alchemist." Over his grave in Westminster Abbey are the words, " O rare Ben Jonson." He was assisted in his early dramatic career by Shakespeare, and he was at one time the traveling tutor to the son of Sir Walter Raleigh.

121. Before the Restoration the parts of women had been played by young men. This explains the frequency with which the old dramatic authors disguised their heroines in male attire.

122. Pedro Calderon de la Barca, 1600–1681, one of the most celebrated of Spanish playwrights and poets. He wrote more than a hundred plays.

123. Viola is the charming heroine of " Twelfth Night "; Alceste, the hero of " Le Misanthrope," is a high-minded though unreasonable gentleman; Agnès, in " L'École des Femmes," is the type of the utterly unsophisticated young girl.

124. Thomas Southern, 1660–1746, British dramatist. His most popular play was " Isabella, or the Fatal Marriage," which Mrs. Siddons revived, and in which she made her first success forty years after his death.

125. Thomas Otway, 1651–1685, the principal tragic poet among the English dramatists of the seventeenth century. His most famous play was " Venice Preserved." See note 94.

126. Thomas Shadwell, 1640–1692, playwright and poet laureate, is better remembered by the sharpness with which he was satirized by Dryden in " MacFlecknoe " and in the second part of " Absalom and Achitophel " than for anything he himself wrote. Dryden said of him :

> " The rest to some faint meaning make pretence,
> But Shadwell never deviates into sense."

His plays, however, although they were exceedingly coarse, were not without wit.

127. Juvenal, about 60–140, a noted Roman satirist.

128. Lucretius, died 55 B.C., a Roman philosophical poet. His great poem, " De Rerum Natura " (" On the Nature of Things "), treated of physics, psychology, and ethics. Mrs. Browning says of him :

> " Lucretius — nobler than his mood:
> Who dropped his plummet down the broad
> Deep universe, and said, ' No God,'
> Finding no bottom : he denied
> Divinely the divine, and died
> Chief poet on the Tiber side
> By grace of God!"
>
> *A Vision of Poets.*

129. Verulamian doctrine, the theories of Francis Bacon, Baron Verulam. Bacon endeavored to reform the methods of scientific investigation. His service to science was of value, but overestimated at the time of which Macaulay writes. It is of course absurd to suppose that the verse quoted from Dryden was written to be taken literally.

130. Prince Rupert, 1619–1682, nephew of Charles I, commander of the cavalry and afterward of the navy in the war between Charles and Parliament. After the Restoration he came again into power in the British navy. His later years were given to scientific investigation, and he is said to have invented " Prince Rupert drops."

131. John Evelyn, 1620–1706, English author. His diary, first published in the present century, gives most interesting information concerning his time. He devoted many years to the study of gardening, and wrote much upon the subject. See note 45.

132. Hippocrates, a Greek physician, died about 377 B.C. Galen was also a Greek physician, dying about 200 A.D. Both left numerous writings, and for centuries it was held that whatever did not agree with the doctrines of Hippocrates and Galen must necessarily be incorrect.

133. Robert Boyle, 1627-1691, Irish chemist and natural philosopher, best known as the discoverer of Boyle's law of the elasticity of air. Sir Hans Sloane, 1660–1752, Irish naturalist. He succeeded Sir Isaac Newton as president of the Royal Society. His most important book was one upon the natural history of the island of Jamaica. His library of 50,000 volumes and over 3000 manuscripts formed the nucleus of the British Museum.

134. The intellectual energies of the Middle Ages were largely expended in controversies upon obscure points of logic and of theology. Two principal parties were distinguished among the learned men of Europe, — those who followed the teachings of Duns Scotus, and those who adhered to the school of Thomas Aquinas. The first was a Scotch Franciscan friar. Scotus was probably the most clever thinker of the Middle Ages, and yet from a corruption of his Christian name, first used in praise and afterwards satirically, comes our word "dunce." He died 1308. St. Thomas Aquinas, sometimes called the father of moral philosophy, was an Italian, a monk of the Dominican order. He died 1274.

135. Sir Christopher Wren, 1632–1723, one of the most celebrated of English architects. After the Great Fire of London he was at the head of the reconstruction of the burned district, and designed many of the chief churches. St. Paul's Cathedral is his work, and bears on its north door the inscription in his memory: "Si monumentum requiris, circumspice" (If you seek his monument, look around you).

136. Louis XIV of France, called "Le Grand." See note 20.

137. Sir Peter Lely, 1618–1680, court painter to Charles II. A large number of his portraits of court beauties are to be seen at Hampton Court.

138. Count Anthony Hamilton, 1646–1720, was a French author of Irish descent. He was brother-in-law to the Comte de Gramont, a French nobleman of the court of Louis XIV, and afterward of Charles II. Hamilton wrote the "Mémoires" of Gramont, which are very scandalous, but full of information about the fashionables of the court of Charles.

139. Sir Godfrey Kneller, 1646–1723, the contemporary and rival of Lely. His best portraits were of men, especially a series of portraits of English admirals.

140. William Howard Stafford, 1612–1680, was accused by Oates of complicity in the Popish Plot (see note 100) and executed. Stafford was a man of high personal character, and his protestations of innocence were generally believed. His death marked the beginning of the reaction against Shaftesbury.

141. Lord William Russell, 1639–1683, was executed upon the charge of being implicated in the Rye House Plot, a conspiracy formed after the failure of the Exclusion Act to murder the king and the Duke of York.

142. The state of the English prisons continued to be a horrible scandal until the end of the last century, when they were reformed, chiefly through the noble efforts of John Howard, the great philanthropist. When Howard examined the prisons in 1774, he found " no separation preserved between the sexes, no criminal discipline enforced. Every jail was a chaos of cruelty and the foulest immorality, from which the prisoner could escape only by sheer starvation or the jail-fever that festered without ceasing in these haunts of wretchedness."

www.ingramcontent.com/pod-product-compliance
Lightning Source LLC
LaVergne TN
LVHW091256080426
835510LV00007B/291